# CLAIM
## THE
# LEAD

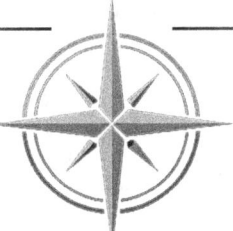

## TRANSFORMATIONAL
## LEADERSHIP
## FOR INSURANCE
## ADJUSTING MANAGERS

### DR. KARISSA THOMAS

Efficient Adjuster Publishing

For permissions, licensing, or bulk purchases, please contact:
Efficient Adjuster Publishing
www.efficientadjuster.net
contact@efficientadjuster.net

Printed in the United States of America
Publisher: Efficient Adjuster Publishing
LCCN: 2025909272
ISBN 978-1-968277-96-3

# Acknowledgments

This book was forged in the fire of real experience—long surge seasons, late-night debriefs, quiet moments of doubt, and powerful conversations that reshaped how I viewed leadership in the insurance adjusting world.

To every adjuster who ever felt unseen while carrying the weight of a claim—your resilience inspired these pages. To the managers and field leads who led with steadiness, even when systems fell short—thank you for modeling what's possible.

To my colleagues, peers, and mentors in the field—you know who you are. Your honesty, grit, and perspective challenged me to write something useful, not just polished. To those who told me their stories, whether over coffee or in catastrophe zones, your trust is not taken lightly.

To the leaders who encouraged professional development and to the firms who believed in training the person behind the metrics—this book is a product of that belief.

And to every reader—thank you for choosing to lead differently. I see you. I honor your commitment to doing hard things with heart.

# Contents

**Conclusion**

# Author's Note

I didn't write this book because leadership is easy.

I wrote it because it is hard—and because in the world of insurance adjusting, it is often invisible. Most leadership books speak to executives or entrepreneurs. Few speak directly to the people managing policyholder heartbreak, juggling metrics, and carrying the emotional weight of high-pressure environments where clarity is rare, but responsibility is constant.

Claim the Lead was born from that gap.

It's for the adjusters promoted for their performance but never trained to lead others. For the team leads who carry their people with care but wonder who is carrying them. For the managers holding up departments under pressure—without recognition, without rest.

It's also born from my own story.

I've been in the field, in the storm, in the seat where leadership must be earned—not assumed. I've led surge teams, trained new leaders, rebuilt broken systems, and sat in silence after hard calls. I've worked in spaces where leadership meant holding a standard with one hand and someone else's burnout in the other. I've witnessed teams break under poor leadership—and rise under the right one.

This book is my offering back to the profession and people who shaped me.

It is built on the four Claim the Lead™ Leadership Pillars:

**Clarity**, to remove ambiguity and anchor expectations.

**Culture**, to create environments where people thrive.

**Coaching**, to develop performance through trust, not control.

And **Emotional Presence**, the steady leadership trait no metric can measure—but every team needs.

Leadership in adjusting isn't glamorous. It's granular.

It happens in missed notes, quiet pauses, difficult conversations, and small decisions made when no one else is watching. It lives in your tone. Your timing. Your ability to stay human under pressure. These moments don't show up in dashboards—but they shape your team, your reputation, and your legacy.

This book names what often goes unsaid:

That leadership here is lonely.

That metrics without meaning are dangerous.

That coaching without care burns people out.

And that you can be strong without being harsh—and firm without losing heart.

I didn't write this book to make leadership sound easy. I wrote it so you could see yourself more clearly in the hard.

Because your leadership is not small. It is shaping culture claim by claim, file by file, voice by voice.

This isn't a manual. It's a mirror, a map, and a moment to reset.

You don't have to lead like the person before you. You don't have to lose yourself to maintain authority. You just need alignment—between who you are, what you value, and how you lead under pressure.

This industry is changing fast. But leaders like you—leaders who choose presence over pressure—are shaping what comes next.

*Claim the Lead* is here to walk with you, chapter by chapter, as you build a new standard of leadership in this profession.

Let's begin.

# Introduction

## Claiming the Lead in a Complex Industry

The world of insurance adjusting is dynamic, demanding, and constantly evolving. At the center of every claim is not just a policy, but a person—someone navigating loss, confusion, or disruption. Adjusters step into that space not only to assess damage but to create clarity. They serve as interpreters of policy, witnesses to events, facilitators of resolution, and often the human face of a company during someone's worst moment.

That makes adjusting deeply human work. And because it is human work, it requires human leadership.

### Where Leadership Happens

Leadership in this industry doesn't happen from behind a desk or within a dashboard. It happens in motion—during file reviews, debrief calls, catastrophe deployments, difficult coaching conversations, and the small, consistent moments when someone on your team is looking to you for steadiness. It's not just about what you decide, but how you decide. How you listen. How you respond when tension rises. The tone you set—without saying a word.

There are no headlines celebrating middle managers in claims. But that's exactly where the culture lives or dies. Where morale rises or falls. Where trust is built—or quietly erodes.

Leadership in adjusting isn't a role you hold. It's a responsibility you carry—one that blends operational excellence with emotional presence.

## Why This Book Exists

Claim the Lead was written for leaders in the thick of it. Not consultants. Not distant executives. But the leaders guiding their teams through policy confusion, long nights, deployment surges, staffing challenges, and shifting expectations. Leaders stretched not by incompetence, but by care. Leaders who coach while documenting, motivate while tracking metrics, and carry emotional weight no spreadsheet ever sees.

Whether you're new to leadership or deep into your journey, this book is for you. It doesn't offer scripts or formulas—it offers language, insight, and frameworks you can adapt to your style. More than that, it reminds you: the work you do, though often thankless, is transformative.

## From Management to Meaning

You already know how to manage files. You've trained others to do it. But leadership calls for something different. Vision. Consistency. Emotional clarity. It calls you to think not just about tasks, but about tone, trust, and trajectory. To shape spaces where people grow, succeed, and occasionally stumble—without fear.

Because in this field, what matters is not just what gets done, but how people feel while doing it. Do they feel seen? Safe to speak up? Clear on what matters and why it matters? Are they being developed—or just managed?

These aren't bonus questions. They're leadership questions.

## What You'll Find Here

Throughout this book, we explore how to lead with presence instead of pressure. How to coach rather than control. How to communicate across generations, personalities, and time zones. How to build resilient teams without burnout. How to hold people accountable without losing trust. And how to adapt to change without abandoning your values.

We'll name the harder truths as well. We will explore what it feels like to be undermined, how to lead when no one is developing you, the quiet exhaustion of always being steady for others, and the decisions you must make when your own leadership spark begins to fade.

These chapters aren't checklists. They're a conversation. A mirror. A map.

## How the Book is Structured

We begin with the realities of the adjusting environment—because leadership doesn't exist in a vacuum. From there, we build on foundational shifts: mindset, communication, emotional regulation, and team culture. Next comes performance, motivation, and systems that drive sustainable success. Then we turn toward the future—leading in a tech-driven world, developing other leaders, and responding to disruption with emotional steadiness.

In the final section, we go deeper: exploring the inner life of a leader, how to lead through fatigue or conflict, and what it really means to stay grounded in a system that doesn't always reward your humanity.

Each section ends with reflection prompts to help you apply what you've read—not as a task, but as a practice. Use them with your team, in 1-on-1s, or in moments when leadership feels heavy.

## What This Book Asks of You

This book isn't asking you to become someone else. It's asking you to bring more of who you truly are—your steadiness, clarity, thoughtfulness, and courage—into every interaction, system, and culture you influence.

You don't need to lead like the person before you. You don't need to move faster, talk louder, or carry more than you should. What you need is alignment. A clear voice. And a way of leading that reflects your values—not just the volume of your inbox.

Because you shape how people experience this work. How they feel. How they grow. And whether they stay.

That impact isn't small. It's everything.

Now it's time to claim it.

## Recommended Companion Resource

While *Claim the Lead* empowers you to coach, develop, and align claims teams, many adjusters still need guidance in the day-to-day communication that defines the role.

For practical tools on empathy, tone, emotional intelligence, and boundary-setting, explore:

## Communicate, Connect, and Lead:
## A New Standard for Insurance Adjusters

This essential guide is the perfect complement to *Claim the Lead*, created for adjusters working in high-pressure environments where clarity and care must go hand in hand.

Available on Amazon and through Efficient Adjuster™.

# Part 1

## Foundations of Leadership in Adjusting

### Reclaiming Your Voice in a Pressure-Filled Industry

Before leadership can inspire excellence, it must first acknowledge reality. In the world of insurance adjusting, that reality is often chaotic, metric-driven, and emotionally charged. Adjusters are expected to perform at high levels while carrying emotional labor that is rarely named and often misunderstood.

In this environment, leadership can become either a source of steadiness—or an added layer of strain.

This section is your reset.

It's where we strip away outdated assumptions about leadership as control or correction and begin rebuilding it on the foundation of clarity, presence, and emotional integrity. These early chapters don't offer formulas—they offer frameworks. They invite you to stop managing from reactivity and start leading from alignment.

Whether you're stepping into leadership for the first time or recalibrating after years in the role, this is your invitation to reclaim your voice—not as a taskmaster, but as a culture shaper, capacity builder, and emotionally attuned leader.

Because when leadership becomes human again, everything changes.

# Chapter 1

## The Harsh Realities of the Claims Environment

> *"Leadership doesn't begin with a title—it begins the moment you decide to take responsibility for the energy you bring into the room."* — Dr. Karissa Thomas

To understand the kind of leadership insurance adjusting truly needs, one must first grasp the environment in which adjusters are asked to work. By its very nature, this environment is intense. The work is emotionally charged, highly regulated, and relentlessly fast-paced. Each claim involves an individual navigating a loss, and behind every file is a phone call, a policyholder, a policy interpretation, and a decision that carries weight. For many adjusters, that weight builds—and without the right leadership, it can become overwhelming.

### The Pressure Behind the Metrics

Claims departments often have rigid hierarchies and metric-driven mindsets. Adjusters on the front lines handle increasingly complex work while meeting sometimes unrealistic expectations. They must balance policyholder empathy with cost control, compliance with customer satisfaction, and speed with accuracy—all within a limited timeframe.

In many organizations, those expectations are passed down with little consultation from the people doing the work. Decisions are made from the top, and adjusters are expected to adjust—not just claims, but also to evolving processes, inconsistent communication, and shifting systems. The result is an environment that can feel both isolating and pressure-filled. Without strong, emotionally intelligent leadership to bridge that gap, the system begins to strain.

## The Invisible Weight

What often goes unseen is the emotional labor adjusters carry. Every day, they speak to people at their most vulnerable—after a car accident, a house fire, a flood, or a theft. They are expected to remain calm, helpful, and composed even when the claimant is angry, fearful, or frustrated. They manage not only the technical aspects of claim resolution but also the emotional fallout of loss.

Add to this the weight of tight deadlines, performance quotas, limited resources, and the ever-present fear of making a mistake, and it becomes clear why burnout is so prevalent in this profession. Many adjusters enter the industry with care and precision, only to find themselves drowning in volume and bureaucracy months or years later. High turnover is often a symptom—not of weak will—but of a system that has failed to value and support the people who keep it running.

## The Erosion of Trust

The truth is that much of what goes wrong in claims culture stems from a lack of trust—adjusters who don't feel trusted to use their judgment, teams that don't feel safe offering feedback, and leaders who may not realize how deep the disconnect has become. Without that trust, a kind of quiet disengagement sets in. People stop raising concerns. They stop going the extra mile. They protect themselves from the pressure, but in doing so, they lose their connection to the work.

Burnout in the industry isn't hypothetical—it's pervasive. A 2025 study by Liberty Mutual and Safeco revealed that 50% of independent insurance agency employees report feeling burned out, with 87% noting increased workloads over the past year and over half feeling overwhelmed by the demands. These statistics aren't just numbers—they are warning signs. Leaders who ignore them risk overseeing teams that are physically present but emotionally absent. Leadership, in this environment, isn't optional—it's the only safeguard against widespread disengagement.

## What Still Works

It's not all broken. There are teams that thrive, adjusters who grow, and leaders who inspire. But those environments don't happen by accident. They are built intentionally—by leaders who understand that performance and well-being are not in opposition. By leaders who know that meeting metrics is not the same as building a sustainable, motivated team. And by leaders who see their role not as enforcing rules, but as shaping a culture that honors both people and results.

Leadership in this space is not about stepping in only when things go wrong. It's about staying present enough to notice when someone is struggling, being curious enough to ask the right questions, and having the courage to challenge the systems that cause unnecessary harm. It's about bringing a steady hand to a profession that demands both heart and resilience.

## Grounding Before Growth

This chapter is not meant to be discouraging; it's meant to be grounding. Before we can talk about transformation—before we can discuss leading differently—we must be honest about what we're leading through. The claims environment is challenging, but it is also full of possibility. When adjusters are supported well, they don't just process claims; they become trusted professionals who serve with accuracy, integrity, and compassion.

In the chapters ahead, we will begin the real work of building that kind of leadership—starting with the mindset shift from doing the work yourself to empowering others to perform it effectively.

## 🔭 Looking Ahead

The next chapter explores what it means to lead beyond your individual performance. We'll examine the foundational mindset shift from doing the work yourself to developing others—redefining success not as personal output, but as the culture, clarity, and confidence you build in your team.

---

### 🔍 Leadership Reset Prompts — Chapter 1: The Harsh Realities of the Claims Environment

*Take a moment to reflect on the emotional and operational truths of the environment you lead in. These prompts are not just for awareness—they're a call to reconnect with what your team actually needs and to ground your leadership in empathy, steadiness, and practical wisdom.*

- *What emotional or operational pressures are most affecting my team right now—and how have I been responding?*

- *Where in our culture has silence replaced feedback or trust?*

- *How can I show up with more presence—not pressure—for someone on my team this week?*

- *What one truth about the claims environment do I need to acknowledge more openly in my leadership?*

---

# Chapter 2

## The Foundation of Effective Leadership

> *"The hardest part of leadership isn't the work—it's the identity shift required to see yourself as more than a task manager."* — Dr. Karissa Thomas

Leadership in insurance adjusting has evolved. It's no longer sufficient to be a high-performing adjuster who knows how to close files quickly or interpret policy with technical accuracy. That kind of success may lead to a promotion—but it won't sustain your leadership. Today's adjusters face emotional pressure, digital overload, high expectations, and increasingly complex claims. They seek more than a supervisor who can correct their documentation. They want a leader who knows how to guide people.

That shift—from doing the work to leading others through it—is one of the hardest transitions in a claims professional's career. It requires more than a new title or access to reporting dashboards; it demands a complete reorientation of mindset. Where once your value was tied to your own precision, speed, and independence, now your value is measured by your ability to influence others, build trust, and make decisions that serve the whole—not just your own success.

At first, that shift can feel jarring. Many new leaders carry their old instincts into their new roles, often hovering over files or jumping into resolutions too quickly. Not because they're controlling—but because they know how to fix things. They've done the work before. But leadership isn't about being the best adjuster in the room. It's about creating an environment where others can excel. It's about knowing when to step back, when to challenge, when to guide, and when to let someone make a mistake that will help them grow more than your correction ever could.

## Introducing the Claim the Lead™ Leadership Pillars

This is where the Claim the Lead™ Leadership Pillars come into play—a framework that grounds leadership in the practical needs of adjusting teams while supporting long-term culture and performance.

These pillars include:

- **Clarity** — removing ambiguity so people can act with confidence.
- **Culture** — shaping daily experiences through trust, tone, and behavior.
- **Coaching** — developing talent through intentional support, not control.
- **Emotional Presence** — the foundation of all leadership decisions: being steady, aware, and engaged, even under pressure.

These four pillars will surface repeatedly throughout this book. They're not separate from performance—they are the foundation that makes performance sustainable.

## Influence Over Expertise

You'll always need technical knowledge in this field. Understanding policy interpretation, regulatory shifts, and documentation expectations will always be important. However, a leader who relies solely on technical expertise will eventually hit a ceiling. At some point, knowledge must give way to influence. It must give way to people.

Leadership in adjusting involves learning to read the room, not just the file. It requires understanding when someone on your team is overwhelmed but hesitant to speak up. It demands knowing how to ask better questions rather than offering quicker solutions. Additionally, it entails being able to manage your own response when your team's performance or behavior triggers feelings of frustration, disappointment, or insecurity.

Such leadership cannot be faked; it must be practiced.

## Emotional Awareness and Team Performance

Over time, great leaders develop emotional awareness without becoming emotionally reactive. They become technically sharp without being rigid. They learn to stay grounded in their values, even as the systems, goals, and tools around them shift.

As you grow in your leadership, you'll also need to develop a new relationship with performance. Not just with your team's output, but with the culture surrounding how that output is created. Are people racing through claims, or taking pride in quality? Are they motivated by shared goals, or driven by fear of correction? Are they staying because they believe in what they're building, or because they don't think they have a better option?

These are the indicators that matter: not just cycle time, but team tempo; not just QA scores, but how people feel when they come to work each day. A high-performing team is not only one that delivers results—it's one that can sustain those results over time without emotional erosion.

## Hiring for Culture, Not Just Competence

This begins with how you engage people.

Hiring is more than just filling gaps; it's inviting someone into the ecosystem you're shaping. While technical aptitude can be taught, presence and communication often cannot. A great hire isn't just someone who meets the metrics; it's someone who can collaborate under pressure, receive feedback without defensiveness, and remain calm when policyholders escalate. Look for indicators of judgment, compassion, and personal accountability, as those are the qualities that shape culture, not just caseloads.

## Growth Through Development, Not Pressure

But even the best hires will stall in growth without intentional development. Strong leaders prioritize learning, not just for the sake of compliance, but because they understand that investment in growth creates stability. The strongest teams are not only well-trained—they're well-supported. This means regular feedback conversations, not just annual reviews. It involves creating space for curiosity and improvement without micromanaging. Furthermore, it means establishing systems where development isn't something squeezed in "when things slow down"—but integrated into the normal rhythm of leadership.

## Culture Is Built in the Details

Of course, even the most talented team cannot perform well in a culture that lacks clarity or care.

Leadership is ultimately about culture-building. It's the tone you set in meetings, how you respond when a mistake occurs, and the consistency with which you reinforce expectations. Culture isn't found in posters or policies; it exists in everyday interactions—especially under pressure.

What are the unwritten rules your team follows? What gets rewarded? What gets overlooked? What are the non-negotiables? What habits do you allow to go unaddressed because they're easier to ignore than confront?

These are leadership questions—not philosophical but practical ones. Your culture doesn't emerge from your intentions; it emerges from your habits, from what you model, what you tolerate, and what you reinforce.

## From Managing to Multiplying

And when you get it right, something powerful occurs.

Your team doesn't just perform; they take ownership. They think for themselves while remaining aligned with your standards. They hold each other accountable—not because you're watching, but because they care. They come to you not just with problems but also with ideas, awareness, and initiative.

That's not accidental. It's the result of foundational leadership. The kind that doesn't need to prove itself—but shows up consistently. The kind that adapts to the team without lowering the bar. The kind that knows success is not just hitting numbers, but building people.

As you continue building from here, let this serve as your reminder:

Your team is watching you—not only for answers, but for your presence. Not merely for knowledge, but for stability.

The type of leader you are is not defined by how much you do—it's defined by what you're willing to build.

What you build begins now.

## 🔭 Looking Ahead

In the next chapter, we'll look at the evolving role of the claims manager. You'll learn how to lead in motion—balancing systems, people, and presence in a fast-paced, pressure-filled industry. Because great leadership doesn't just influence outcomes—it shapes the entire environment in which those outcomes happen.

## 🔍 Leadership Reset Prompts — Chapter 2: The Foundation of Effective Leadership

*Reflect on your current mindset and habits as a leader. These questions are designed to help you assess how your leadership influences culture, development, and emotional clarity across your team.*

- **What outdated habits or instincts from my time as an adjuster am I still bringing into my leadership?**

- **Where have I confused technical excellence with leadership effectiveness?**

- **Am I reinforcing clarity, coaching, and culture—or just managing output?**

- **What do I want the emotional climate of my team to feel like, and what am I doing to shape it daily?**

# Chapter 3

## The Role of a Manager in Insurance Adjusting

> *"Your tone is your leadership. Every conversation is a chance to build or break trust."* — Dr. Karissa Thomas

To manage in the world of insurance adjusting today is to lead in motion. The landscape isn't static—it's shifting beneath your feet. Technology is advancing, workflows are decentralizing, and customer expectations are evolving. Managers are no longer simply overseeing claims or enforcing procedures. They are coaching teams through rapid change, guiding them through conflict, and setting standards in environments that often feel uncertain or overstretched.

What once defined a manager—a sharp technical mind, the ability to work quickly, and the know-how to resolve complex claims—now represents only one aspect of the role. Today's claims leaders must move beyond subject-matter expertise and engage in the deeper work of leadership: shaping culture, protecting performance, and anchoring their teams in clarity when so much feels uncertain.

## From Bottlenecks to Builders

And this shift matters because, without it, managers become bottlenecks. They remain mired in the weeds, caught in the tension between doing and leading, responding and designing. However, when a manager recognizes the scope of their influence—and owns it—they transition from merely managing outcomes to actively shaping the environment in which outcomes are possible.

## Translators of Trust and Performance

Leading in this field now requires fluency in both systems and people. You must understand claims regulations, compliance protocols, and the rationale behind file documentation. However, you also need to sense when your team is burning out, when someone is avoiding difficult conversations, or when a policyholder requires more reassurance than direction. You serve as the translator between performance metrics and human experience.

It's not easy to strike a balance—especially in remote or hybrid teams. The old model of leadership relied on visibility. You could walk the floor, check in informally, and spot tension before it exploded. Now, leadership depends more on intentionality than proximity. It's about creating rhythms and touchpoints that replace what once happened organically: one-on-one check-ins, Slack messages that ask not just for updates but for insight, and team meetings that don't just cover numbers but surface needs.

## Technology as Tool—and Tension

Technology plays a role in all of this—both as a tool and a pressure point. Claims automation, AI-supported documentation, and digital communication platforms have changed the rhythm and expectations of work. The systems that once supported the work are now often driving it. Leaders must help their teams navigate this landscape—not with fear, but with clarity. Not every tool is intuitive. Not every process improves efficiency at first. Part of your job is to create space for learning, frustration, and adaptation. To say, "Yes, this is new. And we'll figure it out together."

That's what leadership in this space now demands—a posture of learning and leading simultaneously. Because the answers aren't all present. And that's okay. The role of the manager is not to always be right—but to always be responsive. To notice patterns, ask better questions, and support better decisions.

## The Enduring Needs of Adjusters

And while the work is shifting, the core needs of adjusters remain steady. They still want to be recognized, to be developed, and to be trusted. They want to know where they stand, what's expected of them, and how to grow. Managers who meet those needs consistently—not just through performance reviews, but through daily interaction—build teams that thrive. They create environments where people feel grounded enough to take risks and secure enough to ask for help.

## Building Legacy Through Leadership

Succession becomes a natural outgrowth of this kind of leadership. When you manage well, you're not just holding a team together—you're preparing others to lead. You're creating depth. Your influence doesn't end when someone gets promoted or moves to another team; it carries with them, built into the way they now lead others.

This role is significant; it's foundational. Managers set the tone for how leadership is experienced on a daily basis. You don't need to be a VP to create cultural impact; you need to be present, consistent, and human. When the people closest to the claim feel supported by their leaders, everything changes—how they speak to policyholders, how they document decisions, and how they carry themselves under pressure.

You are not merely managing claims. You are managing trust, momentum, and potential. And you are doing it in one of the most nuanced, fast-paced, and emotionally complex fields there is.

## The Claim the Lead™ Leadership Pillars (Revisited)

Effective leadership in insurance adjusting doesn't rely on titles or tenure—it hinges on four core pillars that shape team performance, emotional health, and long-term resilience. This framework, called the Claim the Lead™ Leadership Pillars, reflects what teams need most in high-pressure, emotionally demanding environments:

- **Clarity** removes guesswork and empowers confident action. It ensures that expectations, standards, and feedback are shared openly—not left to assumption or interpretation.
- **Culture** is what your team experiences every day— through tone, trust, and behavior. It is shaped not by what is said, but by what is modeled, reinforced, and allowed.
- **Coaching** is where transformation happens. Instead of managing from a place of control, coaching develops others through belief, feedback, and intentional growth.
- At the center of these three pillars is the quality that holds them all together: **Emotional Presence**—the leader's ability to stay grounded, responsive, and steady in the face of pressure.

When emotional presence is missing, leadership defaults to reactivity. But when it is present, everything aligns—performance, morale, and trust.

**LEADERSHIP IN ACTION:
THE TURNING POINT IN A STORM TEAM DEBRIEF**

After Hurricane Eliza made landfall, Marcus—a seasoned CAT team lead—was running operations on fumes. The deployment was intense, files were piling up, and the pressure to perform was relentless.

During a team debrief, one adjuster spoke up:

"I know you want us to get it right. But when you come at us with corrections instead of questions, it shuts everything down."

It wasn't an outburst—it was exhaustion finding its voice.

Marcus listened. Then he paused.

The next morning, he pulled the team together and said:

"You're right. I've been managing from pressure, not presence. I want to lead differently. So here's what you can expect from me—more clarity, more coaching, and more ownership for how we shape this culture together."

He didn't lower the bar. He raised the standard for how people should be led.

The result? The team hit their performance goals—and did it without breaking down. They didn't just survive. They grew stronger together.

## Looking Ahead

The next chapter explores how to delve even deeper into this role—transitioning from a task-focused contributor to an influential leader and redefining what leadership looks like in the evolving profession today.

## 🔍 Leadership Reset Prompts — Chapter 3: The Role of a Manager in Insurance Adjusting

*As a leader in motion, your influence is often shaped by how you respond in real time. These prompts are designed to help you reflect on how you're balancing systems, people, and presence—especially in moments of pressure.*

- **Where have I been operating from pressure instead of presence?**

- **Do I have consistent rhythms that help me stay connected to my team beyond metrics?**

- **Am I modeling emotional steadiness—or reacting from urgency?**

- **What's one small change I can make this week to reinforce clarity, culture, or coaching in my daily interactions?**

# Chapter 4

## The Leadership Mindset —
## From Adjuster to Influencer

> *"Culture isn't what you preach. It's what your team experiences on a*
> *Monday morning when things go wrong." — Dr. Karissa Thomas*

Stepping into leadership involves more than just a change in title; it signifies a redefinition of identity.

For many insurance professionals, the path to management is paved with technical excellence. Years of adjusting complex claims, balancing policy language with real-life chaos, and navigating emotionally charged conversations build both skill and credibility. However, once you become a leader, the metrics that once defined success no longer apply in the same way. The work isn't about how well you perform; it's about how well you influence the performance of others.

This shift surprises many new leaders.

You're no longer measured by how quickly you close files or how expertly you handle a policyholder's frustration. Now, your effectiveness is assessed by how well your team functions—how they respond to pressure, how they grow, how they collaborate, and how they represent the company in the moments you're not watching.

## Guiding Without Gripping

It is tempting to carry old habits into your new role—to jump in and fix things, to over-explain, or to quietly pick up the slack when someone falls short. However, leadership is not about doing more; it is about guiding more intentionally. It is about resisting the urge to solve every problem and learning to ask better questions instead. It is about creating an environment where people rise, not because they are being micromanaged, but because they feel trusted, supported, and challenged.

The leadership mindset is rooted in influence—not authority. It reflects in the tone you set, the consistency you model, and the belief you have in people even when they doubt themselves. You become not just a team lead but a culture shaper. You define what's acceptable, what's encouraged, and what's possible.

## The Internal Tension of Growth

This shift can be disorienting at first. The tasks that once gave you confidence may now feel out of reach—not because you can't do them, but because accomplishing them would mean stepping back from your leadership responsibilities. You'll find yourself balancing the urge to step in with the discipline to step back. And in that tension lies your growth.

What your team needs most isn't someone who can fix everything. They need someone who sees the bigger picture, who can connect the dots they can't yet see, and who can hold them accountable with respect, not control.

## Emotional Fluency in Action

This requires emotional steadiness.

Leadership is deeply emotional work, even if the industry doesn't always acknowledge it. It demands that you remain calm when others spiral, to manage your own frustration when performance slips, and to show empathy in moments when you're running on empty yourself. These are not "soft" skills. They are the backbone of sustainable leadership.

Emotional intelligence isn't just a bonus trait—it's a vital leadership tool. Instead of merely listing competencies, consider how it exists within you. When you pause before reacting, when you hold your boundaries with clarity and care, and when you check in with someone—not as a mere checkbox, but out of genuine concern for how they're doing—these are not small acts. They are behaviors that set the culture, and they are learned over time.

## Translating Vision into Clarity

As a leader, you also become a translator. You translate the organizational vision into tangible team goals. You translate pressure from above into purpose below. You translate moments of confusion into opportunities for clarity. The better you become at this translation, the more trust you build—not just with your team, but also with your leadership peers.

That trust is now your currency.

Part of building that trust involves creating a rhythm in which people know how to succeed—not by guessing what you want, but by being clearly aligned with what matters. The more transparent you are about expectations, priorities, and standards, the more empowered your team becomes.

## Leading Across Differences

This mindset also helps you manage different personalities, experience levels, and generations. Some team members may require regular feedback and encouragement, while others may thrive on autonomy. Your leadership becomes most effective when it adapts to meet these needs without sacrificing its own integrity.

In moments of high stress—during surges, system transitions, or difficult audits—your team will look to you less for direction and more for tone. Your ability to stay grounded, to offer clarity without panic, and to model stability will often communicate more than your words. These moments deepen your credibility, not because you had all the answers, but because you remained steady enough to lead through the uncertainty.

## You've Already Begun

You may not always feel prepared for the weight of leadership. However, you're not supposed to feel ready—you're meant to show up, learn, reflect, and adjust. You should grow alongside your team, not ahead of them. Furthermore, you're meant to lead in a way that feels true to you—not like the person who held the role before.

You are not here to replicate someone else's style.

You are here to lead with clarity, humility, and quiet strength of your own.

Take a moment to acknowledge that you've already begun. The very fact that you're reading this—that you care enough to grow—means that leadership has already taken root in you.

From here, your role will be to nurture it, to continue showing up with presence, to choose curiosity over certainty, and to cultivate the kind of influence that empowers others to do their best work—not by pushing them, but by walking beside them.

That mindset changes teams.

That is the leadership that lasts.

**LEADERSHIP IN ACTION: LETTING GO TO LEAD**

When Renée was promoted from adjuster to team lead, she was eager to prove herself. Every file issue, she fixed. Every frustrated policyholder, she jumped in. Every team mistake, she absorbed. At first, her team was grateful—but over time, they became dependent. They stopped taking initiative. They waited for her to step in. And she was burning out.

One day, after working late for the fifth night in a row, she paused and asked herself: "What am I really teaching my team?"

The next morning, she made a different choice. Instead of correcting a new adjuster's report line by line, she asked, "Walk me through your thought process—how did you approach this?"

The adjuster hesitated, then explained. The report still needed revisions, but this time, Renée coached instead of correcting. She listened. She offered insight. And she stepped back.

Weeks later, that same adjuster coached a peer through a similar report.

That's when Renée realized: she wasn't just doing the work anymore—she was building people.

## 🔭 Looking Ahead

In the next chapter, we shift from individual leadership mindset to collective team performance. You'll explore how to build and sustain a high-performance adjusting team—not through pressure, but through alignment, recognition, and the intentional culture you create every day.

## 🔍 Leadership Reset Prompts — Chapter 4: The Leadership Mindset — From Adjuster to Influencer

*This chapter is about the internal shift from performance to presence. Reflect on the identity transition you're navigating and how your mindset is influencing the team around you.*

- *What behaviors or instincts am I carrying into leadership that no longer serve this role?*

- *Where am I reacting from pressure instead of responding with steadiness?*

- *How well am I translating the organization's goals into daily clarity for my team?*

- *In what ways can I lead with more trust and less control this week?*

# Chapter 5

## Building and Sustaining a High-Performance Adjusting Team

> *"What you avoid doesn't disappear. It becomes the culture."*
> — Dr. Karissa Thomas

High performance in claims work is not a product of pressure; it is a product of alignment. The most effective teams are not those that work the fastest or the longest. They are the ones where each member understands the mission, trusts the culture, and takes ownership of outcomes—not because someone is watching, but because they care about how the work gets done.

As a leader, your job is not just to hire capable adjusters; it is to shape an environment where capability turns into consistency and consistency turns into culture. You are not building a group of performers but a team.

### Start With Clarity

That begins with clarity. High-performing teams are not confused teams. They don't guess at what matters or operate in silence. They are grounded in shared language, mutual expectations, and rhythms that make excellence possible. Not every team member will work the same way—but they should understand the same values, speak the same standards, and know what "good" looks like beyond just meeting metrics.

A team performs best when trust is high, systems support the work instead of complicating it, and leaders remain present—not controlling but aware. That awareness allows you to catch misalignment early, course-correct without blame, and coach without eroding morale.

## Culture Beneath the Metrics

And then there's the culture beneath the performance. Because when we adjust, performance without purpose turns into production. Mismanaged production, in turn, leads to burnout.

Excellence isn't the result of exhaustion—it's the product of alignment, purpose, and clear support.

You must create systems that stretch without breaking, and you must safeguard your team's emotional bandwidth as diligently as you protect your company's liabilities. This does not mean lowering the standard; it means constructing the scaffolding that enables people to climb toward it sustainably.

## Recognition That Reinforces Values

This is where recognition plays a deeper role—not as a box to check, but as a reinforcement of values. When someone goes above and beyond, how you acknowledge it tells the rest of the team what matters. When you highlight not just the outcome, but the way the outcome was achieved—with thoughtfulness, empathy, and resilience—you shape not only behavior but also belief.

It's not just about motivating performance; it's about retaining the people who deliver it. Industry leaders like Progressive have shown that investing in leadership development directly impacts retention and team morale. In fact, across the sector, companies that prioritize transparent communication and coaching-centered leadership are experiencing significantly higher retention rates.

When adjusters feel supported, guided, and recognized—not merely managed—they remain. And they bring others with them.

## Accountability Without Fear

Equally important is how you respond when things go wrong. A high-performance culture is not one that avoids mistakes; it's one that learns from them without fear. Your tone during correction sets the emotional temperature of the team. If feedback always feels like judgment, people stop taking risks. If accountability always feels like consequence, people retreat into compliance. However, when your feedback is grounded in care and curiosity, growth becomes part of the norm—not the exception.

## When People Feel Human, They Excel

True performance is never created through pressure alone; it is created through belief. When people feel believed in, they rise. When treated as individuals—not production machines—they offer more than just compliance. They provide creativity, speak up when something feels off, and protect the brand, the team, and the customer experience—not out of fear, but out of pride.

Your role, then, is to cultivate a space where people can show up fully—not perfectly, but with integrity. A space where they are seen for who they are, not just for what they produce. A space where they are encouraged to grow, not merely corrected to conform. A space where performance reflects purpose—not pressure.

Because when people feel human inside the work, they produce results that reflect it.

That is the kind of team that doesn't just meet the mark. It sets a new one.

## Repairing What's Broken

And sometimes, you inherit a team that's already fractured—a team where performance is inconsistent, trust is thin, and culture feels transactional. In these cases, leadership becomes repair work. You can't expect immediate change, but you can expect honesty. Start by naming what's true: what's working, what's not, and what has to shift. Invite people into the rebuilding process. Show them that expectations are changing, but not without support. Some will rise, some won't, but all deserve a chance to be led, not just evaluated.

Culture repair is slow work, but it's worthy work. And when done well, it turns skeptics into stewards.

### LEADERSHIP IN ACTION: TURNING AROUND A TEAM IN TROUBLE

When Darnell stepped in to lead a team with one of the highest attrition rates in the region, he found a group that was technically strong—but emotionally shut down. No one spoke up in meetings. Emails were curt. Feedback was met with silence.

Instead of immediately pushing performance, Darnell spent his first two weeks listening. In one-on-ones, he asked questions no one had posed in months: "What do you need to do your job well? What feels off here?"

He didn't promise quick fixes. But he did make two changes fast: weekly team check-ins to surface unseen issues, and a recognition board celebrating how—not just what—work was being done.

Six months later, not only had the team's performance improved, but their engagement scores climbed too. One adjuster put it best: "We went from surviving to contributing."

That's the power of high-performance leadership grounded in clarity, care, and culture.

## 👀 Looking Ahead

Now that we've explored how to build and sustain a high-performance team, we turn to the communication strategies that keep that performance aligned. In the next section, you'll learn how to lead with clarity, listen with intention, and communicate in ways that strengthen trust—even under pressure.

---

### 🔍 Leadership Reset Prompts — Chapter 5: Building and Sustaining a High-Performance Adjusting Team

*Use these prompts to reflect on your current team culture and the systems you've created—or allowed—to shape performance. High performance starts with leadership presence.*

- *What does "high performance" currently mean on my team— and how is it being defined or reinforced?*

- *Where might clarity, not capability, be the missing ingredient?*

- *How am I recognizing effort, not just outcomes?*

- *What is one element of our culture that needs repair—and how can I begin that process with honesty and support?*

---

# Part 2

## *Mastering Communication for Leadership Success*

Leadership rises or falls on communication.

You can have the strongest strategy and the most capable team—but if your message doesn't connect, inspire, or land with clarity, your leadership loses momentum. In the world of insurance adjusting, where emotions run high and timelines move fast, communication is not a "soft skill." It's the oxygen of leadership. It's how teams stay aligned, how policyholders feel supported, and how trust is built in the moments that matter most.

This section focuses on mastering that kind of communication—not just under ideal conditions, but especially under pressure. Pressure isn't an exception in adjusting; it's the daily context.

You'll learn how to give direction without disconnection. How to adapt your message across roles, personalities, and generations. How to hold space for frustration without losing forward motion. And how to offer feedback in ways that motivate instead of shut down.

When done well, communication becomes more than words—it becomes culture in motion. It's how your leadership is felt, how your values are reinforced, and how your team knows they're not just working—they're being led with intention.

These upcoming chapters will demonstrate how to communicate not just to be heard, but to lead meaningfully—through every conversation you engage in.

# Chapter 6

## Effective Communication Strategies for Adjusters

> *"Control may create compliance, but only trust builds commitment."*
> — Dr. Karissa Thomas

When people think of claims work, they often picture systems, estimates, policies, and procedures. However, beneath all of that—beneath every coverage decision, inspection report, and settlement letter—is communication. It is the skill that threads the entire process together. For leaders, it determines whether the team thrives in alignment or struggles in confusion.

In insurance adjusting, communication is not a background function; it's the core. It builds trust between adjusters and policyholders during emotionally charged moments. It ensures teams remain in sync across shifting caseloads. And it allows leaders to create a sense of stability in environments where timelines are compressed and expectations are high.

### From Transmitting to Translating

Strong communication is not just about what is said—it's also about what is understood. It requires leaders to become translators, not merely transmitters. They must translate priorities, expectations, policies, and emotions. In a high-pressure role, misunderstandings aren't just frustrating—they're costly. They delay claims, create friction, and damage relationships.

And the first place where communication often breaks down is listening.

## Listening as Leadership

Most professionals don't consider listening a leadership skill—but it is. Listening builds trust faster than any motivational speech. It allows the people around you to feel seen. And in the world of adjusting—where much of the work involves navigating someone else's crisis—that validation is everything.

Listening well means slowing down long enough to truly absorb what's being said. It means resisting the urge to respond before the other person has finished. It involves reflecting, paraphrasing, and clarifying, not because you're trying to be perfect—but because you care about getting it right. Great listeners don't just wait to speak. They make the other person feel heard.

### LEADERSHIP IN ACTION: THE IMPACT OF LISTENING

During a particularly tense period of backlogged claims, Leslie, a claims manager, noticed her team was withdrawing. Deadlines were being met, but energy levels were low. Instead of launching another meeting filled with performance reminders, she began each check-in by asking one question: "What's one thing slowing you down right now?"

To her surprise, answers came quickly—system glitches, unreturned vendor calls, and fear of reprimand for minor mistakes. By listening without defensiveness, she unlocked a wave of engagement. The team felt heard, solutions followed, and energy began to shift.

Leslie didn't offer grand speeches. She listened—and everything changed.

## Clarity Over Complexity

But listening is only half the equation. The other half is clarity. In fast-paced environments like claims, communication often becomes abbreviated. Messages are rushed, assumptions are made, and emails become cryptic. Before long, confusion spreads—not because people aren't working hard, but because they aren't aligned.

Leaders must become fervent advocates for clarity. Not excessive detail, but intentional communication. The kind that answers the essential question: What do we need to move forward, and who needs to know?

That means slowing down when it truly matters. It means selecting the appropriate channel—sometimes a phone call is preferable to a message. It means verifying that your instructions are actionable. And it means allowing space for others to clarify without fear of looking confused.

## Tone as a Leadership Tool

One of the most powerful ways to create that space is through tone. How you communicate matters as much as what you say. In high-stress environments, a calm, open tone acts as a leadership tool. It can de-escalate a frustrated adjuster, soothe an anxious policyholder, and reset the energy in a tense team meeting.

This doesn't mean sugarcoating hard truths; it means delivering them with dignity. Saying things like, "I know this won't be easy to hear, but I want to make sure you're informed," or "Here's the decision, and I want to walk through the why together," These statements carry strength—but also emotional intelligence.

## Creating Rituals for Connection

In growing or hybrid teams, communication also serves as a bridge connecting cultures, roles, and even time zones. Leaders must be intentional about reinforcing communication rituals that unite people—even when they work apart. This might involve daily stand-ups, weekly wins shared across the group, and end-of-week wrap-ups that recap the important points. These rhythms prevent people from drifting and foster cohesion without relying on physical proximity.

## Leading Cross-Functional Clarity

Cross-functional communication is another area that deserves greater attention. Adjusters don't work in isolation; they rely on underwriting, claims support, legal, and vendor partnerships. Often, friction between departments arises not from conflicting goals, but from communication gaps.

As a leader, you have the ability—and the responsibility—to model cross-functional clarity. When you involve others, do you provide sufficient context? When you're handing off a file, is it organized? When someone outside your team needs support, are you coaching your team to respond with the same urgency and respect they'd expect for themselves?

Culture is reinforced by how we speak about "them." Leaders who constantly vent about another department unknowingly give their teams permission to do the same. However, leaders who say, "Let's reach out and find a solution," or "We're all working toward the same goal," create a different tone—one that builds bridges instead of walls.

## Repair and Credibility

And when breakdowns occur—and they will—strong communication facilitates repair. A quick follow-up, an honest acknowledgment, and a moment to say, "Let me clarify something I should have said earlier." These small actions don't just fix the issue—they build credibility.

## Emotional Clarity in Practice

Finally, leaders must demonstrate emotional clarity. When your team sees you communicate with both confidence and humility—owning what you know, naming what you don't, and responding to tension with grace—they begin to trust not just your words but also your leadership.

You're not just telling people what to do; you're showing them how to do it well. You're teaching them how to communicate through conflict, provide feedback, and maintain a standard of clarity and presence, even under pressure.

## Looking Ahead

In the chapters ahead, we will explore this further—moving from communication as strategy to communication as resilience. Conflict isn't the exception in adapting; it's the environment. Learning how to lead through it is one of the most powerful communication skills you will ever develop.

## 🔍 Leadership Reset Prompts — Chapter 6: Effective Communication Strategies for Adjusters

*Reflect on the way communication is shaping your leadership and your team culture. These prompts are designed to sharpen your awareness and strengthen your communication habits.*

- **Where in my leadership do I need to listen more—and respond less?**

- **How often do I check for clarity after giving direction?**

- **What tone do I set when the pressure is high—and how can I be more intentional about it?**

- **What rituals or rhythms could I introduce to create stronger communication across my team?**

# Chapter 7

## Navigating Difficult Conversations and Conflict Resolution

> *"Leadership isn't about avoiding mistakes—it's about responding to them with emotional maturity and clarity."* — Dr. Karissa Thomas

Conflict is inevitable. In insurance adjusting, where individuals manage loss, frustration, deadlines, and policy ambiguity, tension is inherent to the work. What distinguishes strong leaders is not their ability to avoid conflict, but their capacity to confront it with steadiness and skill.

For many leaders, difficult conversations are the parts of the job they dread most. They're uncomfortable, unpredictable, and emotionally charged. However, what's even more uncomfortable is the cost of avoiding them. Silence breeds resentment. Misunderstandings deepen. Frustrations simmer beneath the surface until they explode, or worse—slowly drain morale and trust.

Leadership requires the courage to lean in and address issues early, even when it would be easier to let them go, and to do so with care—not blame, but clarity. It's not about controlling the other person; it's about restoring alignment.

## Curiosity Over Control

Every difficult conversation is an opportunity. It's a chance to clarify expectations, rebuild trust, and model what accountability looks like when it's handled with respect. When leaders approach conflict with curiosity instead of reactivity, they change the dynamic entirely. What could have been a defensive standoff becomes a collective effort to understand and move forward.

In conversations with policyholders, this skill becomes even more critical. An upset customer isn't always angry because of the decision itself. Sometimes they're angry because they feel ignored, misunderstood, or dismissed. How we speak to people during those moments—not just what we say, but how we say it—determines whether they escalate further or begin to settle.

There is power in listening without interruption, in reflecting back what you have heard before offering your stance, and in acknowledging someone's experience without automatically agreeing or disagreeing. These subtle shifts hold the key to de-escalating emotionally charged situations.

## Internal Friction and Team Repair

Internally, conflict often manifests as friction among team members, unmet expectations, or the gradual buildup of unexpressed disappointment. Leaders who procrastinate in addressing these dynamics often encounter larger issues that could have been avoided. Conversely, those who intervene early—who identify the tension, foster a space for sincere conversation, and establish a climate of mutual respect—cultivate a culture where individuals do not fear conflict. They learn to navigate it collaboratively.

And that's the real goal—not to eliminate conflict but to enhance the team's ability to manage it effectively.

## Consistency Builds Psychological Safety

Consistency is vital for this. You can't expect people to be transparent with one another if leadership isn't modeling transparency. You can't ask for honest feedback if your own responses are defensive. You can't build trust if your only form of accountability is correction.

It begins with tone, timing, and asking yourself, before entering a difficult conversation, "What outcome am I hoping for here?" If it's just to be right or to unload frustration, the conversation won't build anything. But if it's to understand, to clarify, to align—then it becomes a leadership moment.

## Coaching Through Conflict

When performance issues arise, view them not as disciplinary events but as coaching opportunities. Assume the best. Ask questions and get curious about the barriers before offering a solution. Many underperformance problems stem not from laziness or defiance but from confusion, lack of feedback, or misaligned expectations. If the issue does turn out to be behavioral, the clarity of your communication becomes even more important.

Tough conversations test your presence. Can you remain calm while holding the line? Can you express a concern without demeaning the person? Can you provide feedback without making it personal? These are not just communication skills—they are leadership capabilities that improve with practice.

Over time, your team learns to follow your lead. They begin addressing issues earlier. They feel safe expressing concerns. They take more ownership because they know they won't be shamed— they'll be guided.

Conflict, when managed effectively, becomes a source of strength. It clarifies relationships, reveals what people care about, and invites growth—for the team and for you as a leader.

> ### LEADERSHIP IN ACTION:
> ### THE CONVERSATION THAT CHANGED EVERYTHING
>
> When Serena noticed two of her top adjusters weren't speaking to each other, she felt the tension every time they were in a team meeting. At first, she hoped it would resolve on its own. It didn't.
>
> Instead of ignoring it, she called each one into a private conversation, not to assign blame—but to ask questions. "What's going on from your perspective? What do you need to move forward?"
>
> After hearing them out, Serena facilitated a joint meeting. She set the tone clearly: "We're here to clarify—not to accuse. This team matters more than this tension."
>
> It was awkward. But it was honest. Both adjusters admitted their part. And Serena made space for repair.
>
> Three weeks later, one of them thanked her. "You didn't let it fester. You showed us how to have hard conversations the right way."
>
> Leadership isn't about avoiding friction; it's about demonstrating what maturity looks like in the midst of it.

## 🔭 Looking Ahead

Next, we'll explore how to apply the principles of clear, emotionally intelligent communication in virtual and remote team settings. As adjusting teams become increasingly dispersed, leaders must find new ways to stay connected, set the tone, and reinforce culture—no matter the distance.

## 🔍 Leadership Reset Prompts — Chapter 7: Navigating Difficult Conversations and Conflict Resolution

*These prompts help you reflect on your approach to conflict and identify opportunities to lead with greater steadiness, curiosity, and courage.*

- *What conversation have I been avoiding—and why?*

- *When was the last time I addressed an issue early, before it grew?*

- *How do I typically respond to feedback—and what does that teach my team?*

- *What tone and outcome do I want to bring into my next tough conversation?*

# Chapter 8

## Virtual and Remote Team Communication

> *"Before you judge someone's lack of motivation, ask what in the culture is telling them it's not worth trying."* — Dr. Karissa Thomas

The landscape of work has changed. While field adjusting has long required mobility, the traditional image of a centralized claims office, buzzing with side conversations, quick desk check-ins, and impromptu coaching, has largely faded. Today's claims environment is increasingly remote, hybrid, or dispersed across regions. For leaders, this shift is not just logistical—it's cultural. The heart of that culture still beats through communication.

Leading remotely is not about replicating what worked in the office—it's about reimagining how connection, clarity, and accountability can thrive when you're not in the same room. It involves learning to lead through systems, rhythms, and intention, rather than proximity. It begins with understanding what your team loses when you're not physically present—and how to replace it with something equally powerful.

## Creating Intentional Culture

In traditional settings, culture is often absorbed passively. New hires overhear how a senior adjuster speaks to a policyholder. They observe how meetings are conducted, how tension is handled, and how humor emerges in the break room. In remote settings, those learning moments must be intentionally created. They don't happen by chance—they happen by design.

This is where your presence, even from a distance, becomes critical. Visibility is no longer about walking the floor—it's about creating reliable touchpoints: regular check-ins, thoughtful updates, and structured conversations where team members feel seen, not surveilled. It means showing up on time for a virtual meeting and bringing your full attention, just as you would in person. These moments send a message: "I may not be next to you, but I'm here with you."

## Clarity Over Control

Leaders who succeed in remote environments understand the difference between control and clarity. Remote teams don't need more checklists—they need more context. They need to know what success looks like, what the priorities are, and where to turn when they're uncertain. Additionally, they require the tools to collaborate seamlessly.

Technology plays a role, of course. Platforms like Microsoft Teams, Zoom, and shared claims systems facilitate communication. However, it's not the tool that builds trust—it's how you use it. A well-run team meeting that includes moments of recognition and space for dialogue will be more effective than a dozen disconnected emails. A short, personal message to check in on someone's well-being can have more impact than a status report.

## Reading Energy Across the Distance

Remote leadership also requires a deep understanding of energy. Without the social cues of in-person work, it's easy for team members to disengage quietly. They show up, but they don't lean in. As a leader, your job is to pay attention—to who's withdrawing, who's overwhelmed, and who hasn't spoken up in a while. Not to micromanage, but to reconnect. To ask the question that no report can answer: "How are you holding up?"

---

### LEADERSHIP IN ACTION: A CULTURE CHECK-IN

When Jerome's regional claims team went fully remote, the early weeks were smooth—on paper. Productivity was stable. No one complained. But something felt off.

During a Friday meeting, Jerome paused and asked, "How is everyone really doing—not just with work, but with the shift we've made?"

What followed was unexpected. Adjusters opened up about feeling isolated, unsure of where to turn with questions, and disconnected from one another.

That single moment changed his leadership approach. He introduced weekly wins, a rotating "voice of the week" segment where team members could share tips, and monthly one-on-ones focused on well-being. Engagement rose—and so did trust.

Jerome didn't invent a new platform. He created presence.

---

## Culture in the Everyday

And then, there's culture. Culture isn't just a value on a wall or a theme in an onboarding slide deck. It's how people behave when no one's watching. In remote teams, culture is reinforced through consistency. How you respond to a mistake. How quickly you reply to emails. Whether you allow space for celebration or humor. Whether your tone aligns with your values, even in writing.

The truth is, remote work doesn't make leadership harder—it makes it more visible. It highlights what has always been true: that leadership is about presence, not place; about clarity, not control; about building trust one interaction at a time, even across screens and schedules.

This chapter isn't about mastering digital platforms. It's about mastering the kind of communication that conveys meaning—no matter the distance. Your team doesn't require perfection; they need to know you're consistent, honest, and accessible. They need to feel that you care about the work, but also about them.

## 👀 Looking Ahead

As you close out this section of the book, you have now explored how foundational communication—whether in person, under pressure, or across locations—serves as one of your greatest leadership tools. As we transition into the next phase, we will examine how to convert this communication into momentum—through performance, motivation, and aligned execution that drives results without exhausting your team.

## 🔍 Leadership Reset Prompts — Chapter 8: Virtual and Remote Team Communication

*Use these prompts to evaluate the effectiveness of your remote leadership and how your presence is being felt across distance.*

- **What rhythms or touchpoints have I created to replace in-person connection?**

- **How am I reinforcing culture through consistency—especially in virtual settings?**

- **What's one conversation I could initiate this week to check on team energy?**

- **Is my communication strategy driven by control—or by clarity and care?**

# Part 3

## *Performance, Productivity, and Motivation*

Leadership isn't solely about meeting targets; it's about maintaining excellence while preserving the humanity of your team.

In insurance adjusting, where performance is tracked by the hour and productivity can feel like a moving target, leaders often experience pressure to push harder. However, the strongest teams are not built on pressure—they're built on alignment, clarity, and motivation that transcends metrics.

This section explores how to create systems that empower adjusters to perform with consistency and care. You'll learn how to coach for growth, not just correction. You'll discover how to protect your team's energy while driving results. You'll also gain strategies for recognizing what's working, repairing what's not, and motivating your team without burning them out.

Because when people feel supported—not just monitored—they not only produce more, but also stay longer, grow faster, and lead better.

# Chapter 9

## Coaching and Developing Insurance Adjusters

> *"Standards are not rules—they're reminders of who we're choosing to be, even under pressure."* — Dr. Karissa Thomas

Strong leadership in insurance adjusting doesn't begin with command—it begins with cultivation. The most effective leaders are not necessarily those who know the most or accomplish the most. Instead, they are the ones who recognize potential in others and encourage it with intention and care. They understand that technical excellence is only part of what makes a high-performing adjuster; the rest is learned, shaped, and refined through mentorship, feedback, and steady development.

### Coaching in a Fast-Paced World

In a fast-paced environment, the idea of slowing down to coach may feel like a luxury. Claims keep coming, deadlines must be met, and systems constantly demand attention. However, skipping development in favor of speed is a short-term strategy with long-term consequences. When adjusters learn by trial and error, organizations lose consistency, morale declines, and opportunities for improvement are missed. Coaching is not extra work—it is essential leadership.

The role of a leader is not merely to assign tasks, track metrics, or respond to escalations. It is to cultivate people who are confident, capable, and connected to the mission. Adjusters require guidance not only when they're struggling but also when they're growing. They benefit from consistent feedback, relevant learning opportunities, and the reassurance that their contributions are recognized and supported. Leaders who incorporate development into their routine set a tone that says: "You are not just here to get the work done—you're here to grow."

## Feedback as a Leadership Rhythm

This type of leadership requires more than occasional praise or annual reviews. It demands ongoing conversations. Coaching occurs in one-on-one meetings after a challenging claim. It takes place in the subtle feedback that transforms a mistake into mastery. It is evident in the way we challenge adjusters to think critically, not just follow steps. Leaders who coach consistently build teams that are not only more productive but also more resilient. These teams know how to learn from setbacks, enhance processes, and take ownership of their roles.

## Prevention Through Presence

Coaching also helps prevent performance issues from escalating into crises. Too often, leaders wait until a problem is obvious before they intervene. However, when coaching is integral to the culture, feedback becomes expected, welcomed—even appreciated. Adjusters who receive regular, thoughtful guidance are less likely to feel blindsided when corrections are necessary and more likely to take pride in their progress.

## LEADERSHIP IN ACTION:
## GROWING THROUGH REAL-TIME FEEDBACK

Carlos, a newly promoted supervisor, noticed that one of his adjusters—Jade—was making minor errors in her file notes. While nothing major, these mistakes were consistent enough to impact QA reviews. Rather than wait until the review cycle, Carlos invited Jade for a brief coaching session after a team meeting.

"I'm seeing a pattern I want to help you correct early—because your attention to detail matters. Let's walk through one together."

They reviewed the file, discussed alternatives, and concluded the conversation with a shared goal for improvement.

Two weeks later, Jade's files were not only error-free—they reflected deeper clarity. Carlos didn't wait for a problem to grow. He coached in the moment—and helped Jade rise.

## The Simplicity of Consistent Support

This shift from correction to cultivation doesn't require complex systems; it requires commitment. A simple habit of asking, "How can I support your growth this month?" can open the door to meaningful dialogue. Taking a few minutes to debrief a challenging claim or highlight what was handled well creates learning in real time. Creating space for your team to reflect, share what they're working on, and stretch into new responsibilities—these daily moments weave development into the fabric of your leadership.

## Feedback that Builds, Not Breaks

The tone of your feedback matters as much as the content. When feedback is delayed, vague, or only provided when things go wrong, it creates anxiety rather than promotes improvement. However, when it's offered promptly, clearly, and respectfully, it builds trust. The best feedback connects behaviors to outcomes. It doesn't merely point out what happened—it explains why it matters. Most importantly, it provides a path forward. Adjusters need to understand what success looks like, where they stand in relation to it, and how they can move closer to it—with your help.

## Letting Go to Let Others Rise

Of course, coaching also involves knowing when to step back. Leadership isn't about micromanaging—it's about enabling growth. It entails delegating challenges that stretch people, inviting their ideas, and believing in their ability to rise. It's about perceiving the role not as a gatekeeper, but as a gardener—clearing space, offering support, and trusting the process of growth.

## Development as Culture

When development becomes a part of your culture, everything improves. Claims are handled with greater confidence and care. Adjusters become more engaged, loyal, and creative. Mistakes decrease, innovation increases, and the team begins to evolve together. Perhaps most importantly, leadership transforms from a top-down approach to shared responsibility—because everyone starts taking accountability for each other's growth.

That is the kind of team every leader desires. And it's the kind of team every leader can contribute to building.

## 🔭 Looking Ahead

In the chapters that follow, we will explore how to safeguard that growth by creating systems for time, energy, and efficiency—ensuring that your team can not only grow but thrive.

## 🔍 Leadership Reset Prompts — Chapter 9: Coaching and Developing Insurance Adjusters

*Use these prompts to reflect on how coaching is—or isn't—part of your leadership culture and identify where development can become more consistent, intentional, and empowering.*

- *How often do I provide feedback outside of formal reviews— and how is it received?*

- *What space have I created this month for my team to grow, stretch, or reflect?*

- *Am I offering correction only when something goes wrong— or cultivating improvement regularly?*

- *Where could I delegate responsibility to stretch someone's potential instead of solving the problem myself?*

# Chapter 10

## Time Management and Efficiency in Claims Processing

> *"True leadership is measured not by how you perform when it's easy, but how you respond when everything is on the line."* — Dr. Karissa Thomas

In insurance adjusting, time can feel like both the most precious resource and the most punishing pressure. There are deadlines to meet, calls to return, files to close, and documentation to complete—often all at once. In this reality, leaders constantly navigate the tension between productivity and burnout, efficiency and exhaustion.

The temptation, especially in high-volume seasons, is to simply push harder. Adjusters are expected to work faster, manage more claims, and somehow stay balanced through it all. However, true leadership resists this instinct. Instead of asking, "How can we do more?" it asks, "How can we do what matters most—with less waste, more clarity, and greater sustainability?"

### Focus Over Friction

Time management in claims isn't just about speed; it's also about reducing friction, protecting focus, and ensuring that people are doing the right work—not just more work. The goal is not to run adjusters like machines but to build intelligent systems that support human performance without draining human capacity.

It begins with recognizing where time truly goes. Often, it's not the grand claims or urgent calls that steal productivity—it's the fragmented hours, repetitive tasks, missing tools, or poorly defined processes that chip away at momentum. Leaders who assist their teams in reclaiming those hours—not by pushing harder, but by working smarter—build teams that are not only more effective but also more energized.

## Prioritizing What Matters

Creating structure around priorities is one of the simplest and most powerful changes a leader can implement. Many adjusters start their day by reacting to whatever is the loudest or most recent. However, high-performing teams cultivate habits of intentionality. They understand which claims are critical, which tasks require focus, and what can wait. Leaders reinforce these habits by modeling them—by refraining from sending non-urgent messages during dedicated work hours, by safeguarding deep work time, and by teaching the team how to prioritize their own workload.

## Streamlining Systems

This clarity also applies to the systems that govern their work. When documentation templates, communication tools, or file handoffs are inconsistent, every small inefficiency accumulates. Leaders must routinely ask, "Where is the process slowing us down?" and invite the team into that conversation. Often, those closest to the work have the best ideas for how to streamline it. Listening to them—and acting on what they say—is both a performance win and a morale win.

> ## LEADERSHIP IN ACTION: THE POWER OF DELEGATION
>
> Amira was known for her work ethic, but her calendar was overloaded. As a claims supervisor, she personally reviewed every report, managed onboarding, and responded to all escalations.
>
> After two consecutive weeks of late nights, she paused to map her tasks. Then, she identified three that she could delegate and coached team leads to take them on.
>
> One team lead later stated, "That responsibility made me feel like you trusted me—and I grew because of it."
>
> Delegation was not only a relief for Amira, but also a development opportunity for others.

## Delegating with Purpose

Delegation is another critical element of time leadership. Too many leaders hold onto tasks that could—and should—be handed off. Not because the task is unimportant, but because someone else could learn from it, grow through it, or simply execute it just as well. Delegation is not a sign of weakness; it's a sign that you trust your team and that you are directing your energy where it is most valuable. It allows you to lead more strategically while empowering others to take on greater ownership.

But effective delegation isn't about dumping tasks; it's about transferring responsibility with clarity. It involves taking the time to explain the why, the how, and the expected outcome. It includes checking in without hovering and allowing space for people to make it their own. When done right, delegation becomes one of the most powerful development tools in a leader's arsenal.

## From Reaction to Intention

All of this leads to a bigger shift—from managing time reactively to shaping time intentionally. When leaders execute this effectively, the results resonate throughout the team. Stress decreases. Mistakes drop. Engagement improves. People stop dreading Mondays because they're not drowning by Wednesday. Work becomes more human again—and more productive as a result.

Efficiency is not merely about speed for its own sake; it's about honoring the value of people's time, energy, and focus. It's about removing the obstacles that make competent adjusters feel inadequate or overwhelmed. It's also about teaching the team that excellence doesn't have to compromise their well-being.

## Leading for Sustainability

Strong leaders manage claims. Exceptional leaders manage capacity. They establish rhythms, safeguard focus, and create breathing room—not because they're trying to be lenient, but because they understand that long-term performance requires sustainability.

## 🔭 Looking Ahead

In the next chapter, we will explore how to maintain that performance—not through pressure, but through recognition, alignment, and sustained motivation.

## 🔍 Leadership Reset Prompts — Chapter 10: Time Management and Efficiency in Claims Processing

*These prompts are designed to help you reflect on your team's relationship with time—and your role in shaping it.*

- **What part of our workflow creates the most friction—and how can we simplify it?**


- **Where am I modeling urgency unnecessarily—and where could I model intention instead?**


- **Who on my team could grow through delegation if I let go more often?**


- **What small change could I make this week to protect time, energy, or focus—for myself or for the team?**

# Chapter 11

## Recognizing and Rewarding High Performers

> *"Leadership isn't just vertical—it's relational. Influence moves in every direction."* — Dr. Karissa Thomas

In the midst of deadlines, data, and decision-making, one of the most powerful tools a leader possesses is often the most overlooked: recognition. In the world of insurance adjusting, where much of the work is complex, fast-paced, and emotionally draining, consistent and authentic appreciation isn't just nice—it's essential. It generates energy. It fosters loyalty. And, most importantly, it lets people know they matter.

High performers don't thrive in silence. They don't remain long where their contributions go unnoticed or where only the problems are acknowledged. They want to know that their efforts have meaning, that their work is recognized, and that their growth is valued. This doesn't mean we celebrate mediocrity or lower standards; it means we understand that excellence flourishes where it's nurtured.

## Recognition as Relationship, Not Reward

Recognition is not a reward system—it's a relationship strategy. It's how you let someone know, "I see the way you showed up in that tough call," or "I noticed the care you put into that documentation," or "The way you mentored that new hire—it changed the tone of the entire team." These moments cost nothing, but they mean everything. They create a ripple effect that strengthens performance, increases engagement, and reinforces the behaviors that define your culture.

---

**LEADERSHIP IN ACTION: RECOGNIZING THE INVISIBLE WORK**

Melanie, a property claims team lead, made it a weekly habit to name one act of "invisible excellence" during team calls. One week, she highlighted how Alex stayed on the phone with a grieving homeowner for 45 minutes—not because he had to, but because the claimant needed it.

Melanie's words were simple: "Alex, that wasn't just adjusting. That was human service. And it matters."

The impact? Team morale rose. Others began calling out each other's moments. Recognition became contagious—and culture followed.

---

## Reward Systems Done Right

But reward systems become dangerous when misused. Pay, when tied to performance, should serve as motivation—not manipulation. In some environments, compensation becomes conditional—used as a threat, a pressure point, or a tool for behavioral correction. This erodes trust. People don't feel seen—they feel monitored. And when someone's livelihood is dangled like a carrot, the culture shifts from growth to survival. Leaders must resist this. Pay should reflect value—not fear. Recognition should reinforce belonging, not behavior control.

## Make It Specific and Sincere

Effective recognition isn't formulaic; it's personal, timely, and sincere. It doesn't have to be grand or public, though those can be powerful. A private message, a handwritten note, or a quick word at the end of a meeting can be more impactful than any formal award. The key is specificity: a vague "great job" falls flat. But when you name the action, the impact, and the reason behind it, it becomes a moment of meaning.

As a leader, your job is not just to recognize outcomes—it's to acknowledge effort, growth, and character. When we only celebrate the end result, we risk overlooking the courage it takes to improve, the resilience required to keep showing up, and the thoughtfulness behind how something was done. A culture of high performance is built when recognition encompasses the journey, not just the destination.

## Customize the Investment

But recognition is only part of the equation. Reward matters too—especially when performance consistently exceeds expectations. Leaders who connect recognition to meaningful rewards—whether through choice assignments, leadership opportunities, or even time flexibility—send a message: "We invest in those who invest in us."

That investment must be tailored. Not everyone is motivated by the same factors. Some crave new challenges, while others value time autonomy, learning opportunities, or career advancement. A key aspect of leadership is understanding what inspires individuals and reflecting that in how you acknowledge and support them.

## Align Recognition With Purpose

When recognition is woven into the everyday fabric of leadership, it transforms the team. People become more accountable—not out of fear, but out of pride. They push harder, think more creatively, and support one another because they feel connected to something meaningful. When recognition is paired with aligned goals, it deepens even further.

This alignment is critical. If your team doesn't see how their work connects to something larger—whether it's the customer experience, organizational success, or a broader mission—they may meet targets but still feel disconnected. Your role is to keep drawing those connections. To say, "This task may feel routine, but here's how it impacts our integrity as a company," or, "That detail you caught—it saved someone from a denied claim they didn't deserve." Context creates pride, and pride sustains motivation.

## Daily Posture, Not Quarterly Program

It's also important to recognize that recognition isn't a quarterly initiative; it's a daily mindset. It's how we build trust, loyalty, and resilience in a field that demands emotional stamina. It's how we ensure that our best people don't quietly burn out but stay—because they feel seen, supported, and challenged in the right ways.

And perhaps more than anything, it's how we remind ourselves that leadership isn't just about outcomes; it's about people. When people feel truly valued, they engage with greater heart, clarity, and consistency.

## CE Opportunity: Ethics and Equity in Performance Pay

This chapter offers an opportunity for continuing education (CE) training focused on ethics in compensation. Topics can include:

- The psychological impact of performance-based pay structures

- Equity concerns in incentive distribution
- Balancing recognition with accountability
- Creating reward systems that reflect values and fairness

This can support leadership training and compliance initiatives for claims supervisors and team leads.

## 🔭 Looking Ahead

As you continue to develop your team's capacity and character, remember: recognition isn't a break from performance—it's what sustains it.

In the next section, we will shift our focus to the future—examining how emerging trends, technologies, and ethics transform the role of leadership in insurance adjusting.

---

### 🔍 Leadership Reset Prompts — Chapter 11: Recognizing and Rewarding High Performers

*These prompts help ensure your recognition is purposeful, inclusive, and connected to lasting motivation.*

- *Whose contributions have I overlooked—and how can I acknowledge them this week?*

- *Do our reward systems reinforce fear or fuel pride?*

- *How consistently do I recognize the effort, not just the outcome?*

- *How well does our team understand the bigger picture—and how can I better connect the dots?*

---

# Chapter 12

## Leading Through Chaos and Surge Events

> *"You can't lead people you no longer have the energy to care for—including yourself."* — Dr. Karissa Thomas

In the world of insurance adjusting, chaos is never abstract. It arrives with force—through hurricanes, wildfires, hailstorms, civil unrest, and back-to-back CAT deployments. It tests systems, reshuffles teams, and reveals both the strengths and gaps in your leadership. These aren't hypothetical challenges. They are real, urgent, and deeply human. How you lead in those moments will be remembered long after the crisis subsides.

## Surge Compresses Everything

Surge events compress everything. Timelines shorten. Emotions heighten. Resources stretch. Policyholders become more desperate, and adjusters grow more fatigued. In the midst of it all stands the leader—not as a hero, but as an anchor. They must remain steady when everything around them is moving quickly and fraying at the edges.

What your team needs in these moments isn't perfection—it's presence. It's the confidence that someone sees the whole picture, absorbs pressure from above, and provides guidance with just enough structure to keep things moving without making people feel micromanaged. Most importantly, it's the sense that they aren't alone.

## Communication as the Stabilizer

In chaos, information is gold. When direction is unclear, people fill in the gaps with assumptions, anxiety, and second-guessing. That's why your communication must become more frequent—not more complex, but more intentional. Clear check-ins, end-of-day debriefs, and "Here's what matters today" messages create essential rhythms. These rhythms act like bumpers on a bowling lane; they don't guarantee strikes, but they keep the team from going off course.

But communication isn't just about tasks and updates; it's emotional too. A quick message that says, "I know today was heavy. Thank you for staying focused," is a leadership action. A moment where you tell someone, "You handled that policyholder with grace," is more powerful than any metric. These touches do more than boost morale—they help prevent collapse.

### LEADERSHIP IN ACTION: STEADY IN THE STORM

During Hurricane Rhea, Malik, a field team manager, oversaw 18 adjusters deployed across two states. Files were pouring in. Tensions were high.

Rather than increasing pressure, he instituted a daily 10-minute debrief call. On day four, one adjuster broke down: "I didn't think I could do this. But hearing your voice each night kept me going."

Malik didn't solve every problem, but he created space for steadiness—and that changed everything.

## Recovery Is Part of the Plan

Still, no team can sustain high-pressure performance indefinitely. That's why leading through chaos also requires a recovery strategy. Leaders who treat surges like sprints experience short bursts of productivity followed by long periods of disengagement. However, those who approach it like a marathon—with pacing, breathing room, and intentional recovery—build teams that endure.

What does recovery look like? It begins with acknowledgment. Too often, once the dust settles, leadership moves on to the next operational priority without recognizing what has just occurred. The emotional residue of surge doesn't vanish on its own; it lingers. If left unaddressed, it hardens into cynicism, fatigue, or quiet resentment.

Gather your team. Name what they carried. Reflect on what was learned. Celebrate moments of strength and acknowledge what has been lost or strained. This kind of debriefing isn't a meeting; it's a healing practice. It says, "What you experienced mattered. And so do you."

## Learn, Then Lead Better

It's also an opportunity to enhance your systems. Ask: What didn't work? Where did people feel unsupported? Where did communication break down? The insights you gather post-surge are some of the most valuable you'll ever receive—because they come from lived reality, not theoretical planning.

## Tone Under Pressure

However, emotional leadership during the event itself is just as important as recovery.

Surge exposes leaders. It reveals tone and blind spots. It shows whether your authority stems from trust or habit. Do people follow your direction because they believe in it or because they fear the consequences of questioning you? In high-pressure moments, tone becomes texture. If your team hears panic in your voice, they feel it in their chest. If your feedback is sharp, they absorb that tension. But if you remain calm—not detached, but grounded—you give them permission to do the same.

You can be urgent without being aggressive, clear without being cold, and directive without becoming unapproachable. These are the micro-skills of emotionally intelligent leadership, and in times of chaos, they matter more than ever.

## Protecting the Leader

Finally, let's name something that often goes unspoken: you, as the leader, are human too. You carry the emotional weight of your team's stress, the pressure of upper leadership expectations, and the burden of being the steady one. While your title may say "Manager" or "Director," you're also a person trying to manage your own resilience amid it all.

Take care of yourself. Stay hydrated. Take five minutes to breathe between calls. Write down your frustrations, so they don't spill over into your team. Talk to someone outside the storm who can reflect truth and steadiness back to you. You cannot lead sustainably if your wellness is an afterthought.

## CE Opportunity: Crisis Communication and Surge Recovery Leadership

This chapter presents an ideal opportunity for continuing education (CE) credit courses focused on:

- Emotional intelligence during surge events
- Real-time leadership communication in crisis
- Post-surge debriefing and recovery planning
- Self-regulation and resilience for claims managers

This training could support team leads and supervisors preparing for CAT events or managing long-term high-volume environments.

## A Defining Moment

Leadership during surge events is one of the most challenging and character-shaping tasks you will undertake. It will stretch you, sharpen you, and, if you reflect on it, prepare you for everything that follows.

Because chaos doesn't build leadership; it reveals it.

The way you guide your people through it will become part of both their story and yours.

## 🔭 Looking Ahead

In the next chapter, we will explore how emotional intelligence shapes the way we raise the next generation. You will learn how present parenting, cultural awareness, and emotional modeling contribute to raising emotionally intelligent children—and how your leadership legacy begins at home.

## 🔍 Leadership Reset Prompts — Chapter 12: Leading Through Chaos and Surge Events

*These prompts help you evaluate how you lead during high-stakes events—and how you recover with your team.*

- *How did my tone, presence, or clarity impact my team during our last surge?*

- *What recovery practices have I put in place—or neglected— after high-stress events?*

- *Where do I need more support in maintaining my own steadiness?*

- *What lessons from our last CAT or surge event should become part of our future planning?*

# Part 4

## *The Future of Leadership in Insurance Adjusting*

The insurance industry is evolving—and so must its leaders.

Technology is accelerating. Regulatory landscapes are shifting. Customer expectations are rising. With every change, leaders are called to adapt—not just operationally, but ethically, emotionally, and strategically.

This section prepares you for what's next—not with fear, but with clarity. You'll explore how to lead through uncertainty without losing your integrity. You'll examine how to future-proof your leadership by building scalable systems and nurturing emerging leaders. And you'll reflect on how legacy is not built through control but through consistent, principled action.

The future of insurance adjusting will reward those who can hold both innovation and empathy, as well as precision and presence. These chapters serve as your invitation to lead forward—anchored in what matters most.

# Chapter 13

## Adapting to Industry Changes
## and Emerging Trends

> *"Correction without connection breeds resistance. Coaching
> invites growth through trust."* — Dr. Karissa Thomas

The insurance adjusting landscape is not what it was a decade ago—and it won't be the same a decade from now. Change in this field is no longer occasional; it's constant. Technology is evolving, customer expectations are shifting, and regulatory environments are tightening. For leaders, this presents both a challenge and an opportunity: the challenge of staying relevant and the opportunity to lead with greater clarity, adaptability, and intention.

## Evolving With Intention

At the heart of future-readiness is the willingness to evolve— not reactively, but purposefully. Too often, change is viewed as something to endure, a disruption to manage. However, transformational leaders perceive change as a signpost, providing an opportunity to ask different questions, try better approaches, and abandon systems and habits that no longer benefit the work.

## Technology and Human Judgment

One of the most visible shifts in the industry is the integration of artificial intelligence and automation. Claims that were once reviewed manually are now triaged by algorithms. Damage assessments are improved by photo analysis software. Policyholders receive automated updates before a human adjuster makes contact. These innovations can enhance speed and consistency—but they also raise new questions. What happens when automation overlooks nuance? How do we ensure fairness and accuracy when decisions are influenced by machines? And how do we keep humanity at the center of a process that is becoming increasingly digital?

The answer doesn't lie in resisting technology—it lies in leading through it. Adjusting teams don't need to fear innovation if they feel empowered to use it wisely. Your role is to ensure your team understands the tools available to them, knows when to trust technology, and when to use their judgment to intervene. It's your voice that reminds them that even as systems evolve, empathy, ethics, and discernment remain non-negotiable.

### LEADERSHIP IN ACTION: TRUSTING TECH WITH CAUTION

When Tasha's team started using automated triage software, it improved turnaround time but flagged several straightforward claims as complex. Instead of blaming the system or reverting to manual review, Tasha led a weekly review of flagged cases.

Her message was clear: "Tech helps us—but judgment still leads us."

Over time, her team became more confident—both in the tools and in their critical thinking. Tasha embraced change, helping her team adapt without losing their voice.

## Leading in a Hybrid World

Remote and hybrid work environments signify another shift, not only in logistics but also in how teams connect, communicate, and maintain accountability. Traditional methods such as walking the floor, holding impromptu desk chats, or observing nonverbal cues are no longer available to every leader. Connection now requires intention. Culture must be deliberately designed, not merely assumed. Trust must be fostered through structure, clarity, and meaningful communication.

For many, this transition has created growing pains. However, it has also enabled leaders to reach farther, operate more flexibly, and retain top talent across geographic boundaries. Those who embrace this shift—who learn how to lead without seeing, to manage through systems instead of proximity—are becoming the new standard bearers of leadership agility.

## Rising Customer and Employee Expectations

Meanwhile, customer expectations are rising. It's no longer sufficient to process claims correctly; they must also be handled quickly, clearly, and with genuine care. Policyholders want transparency, updates, and a sense that their concerns are being understood—not just managed. In this environment, the ability to communicate with empathy, explain policy language in simple terms, and take ownership during friction points has become a leadership imperative.

That expectation extends internally as well. Adjusters don't want to be micromanaged, but they do want to feel guided. They seek reassurance that their leaders are invested in their growth and care about their well-being—not just their productivity. As change accelerates, the emotional aspect of leadership becomes even more crucial. The teams that will thrive in this new era are those whose leaders balance innovation with integrity and systems with humanity.

## Ethics in an Automated Age

Then, there are the ethical complexities that accompany advancement. As we incorporate AI into more claims decisions, we assume responsibility for the recommendations made by those systems. Bias in algorithms, privacy breaches, or unclear decision logic can erode trust more rapidly than ever. Leaders must advocate for transparency—not just in how we communicate with customers but also in how we design and deploy the tools we depend on.

## CE Opportunity: Leadership Ethics and Emerging Technology

This chapter presents an ideal opportunity for CE coursework in:

- Ethical implications of AI in claims handling
- Human oversight and algorithmic bias
- Balancing automation with emotional intelligence
- Legal and regulatory shifts impacting leadership decisions

Such training will enable current and aspiring leaders to approach innovation responsibly and lead with confidence through rapid change.

## Culture Over Compliance

Staying compliant in a changing regulatory environment requires vigilance. As laws evolve to keep pace with technology, leaders must ensure their teams are trained, informed, and confident in applying new guidelines. However, compliance doesn't start with rules; it begins with culture. When a team values fairness, accuracy, and responsibility, compliance becomes second nature—not merely a check-the-box task.

## Presence Over Prediction

Leading through change is no longer a specialized skill. It's a daily requirement. But here's the truth: no one is fully prepared for every change that's coming. That's not what makes you a strong leader. What makes you strong is your willingness to stay present, learn quickly, communicate clearly, and guide your team through uncertainty with steadiness and care.

The leaders who will shape the next era of this industry are already doing so. They are listening. They are learning. They are helping their teams navigate new systems while upholding timeless values. They are willing to step into discomfort because they understand what's at stake: trust, loyalty, reputation, and results.

Change may be inevitable, but leadership—true, values-driven, emotionally intelligent leadership—remains a choice. It's a choice you can make each day.

## 🔭 Looking Ahead

In the next chapter, we will explore how this choice becomes increasingly critical when faced with ethical challenges—and how the strongest leaders protect their teams and customers by leading with principle.

## 🔍 Leadership Reset Prompts — Chapter 13: Adapting to Industry Changes and Emerging Trends

*Use these prompts to reflect on how you are leading through innovation and preparing your team for what's next.*

- *How do I help my team navigate uncertainty without losing clarity?*

- *Where have I allowed fear of change to limit innovation?*

- *How am I reinforcing ethics and transparency as we adopt new tools?*

- *What emerging trend do I need to better understand to lead effectively in the next year?*

# Chapter 14

---

## Ethical Leadership and Regulatory Compliance

> *"Exhaustion is not failure—it's feedback. Wise leaders listen before pushing forward."* — Dr. Karissa Thomas

In an industry built on contracts, coverage, and calculation, it's easy to assume that ethics are managed by rules—that as long as we follow the letter of the law, we're doing enough. However, seasoned leaders know the truth: compliance can be taught, but integrity must be cultivated. In claims adjusting, where pressure is high and gray areas abound, integrity is not optional—it's foundational.

## Doing Right—Not Just Doing Things Right

Ethical leadership is not just about what you avoid; it's about what you actively uphold. It is not about perfection—it's about consistency, transparency, and a willingness to take responsibility when the line between right and wrong isn't clearly marked. In environments governed by deadlines, quotas, and competing demands, leaders serve as the compass. They model what it means to do the right thing, even when it's inconvenient and when no one is watching.

At the heart of ethical leadership is trust—both the trust your team has in you and the trust policyholders place in your organization. When that trust is broken, the damage runs deep. One shortcut, one overlooked inconsistency, or one failure to speak up when something feels off—it only takes a moment for confidence to unravel. Rebuilding it takes much longer.

## Modeling Integrity in Daily Practice

That's why ethical leadership must be visible, intentional, and integrated into the everyday language and behavior of your team. This doesn't mean giving lectures on compliance or referencing policy manuals in every meeting. It means telling the truth when it's hard, acknowledging gray areas, and inviting discussion. It requires owning mistakes publicly and demonstrating how to move forward with integrity, not shame.

It also means protecting your team by ensuring they understand their compliance responsibilities—not just in theory, but also in practice. Adjusters are expected to navigate complex legal environments, follow evolving regulations, and make judgment calls that carry significant weight. Without clear training, guidance, and support, even the most well-intentioned professionals can make decisions that put themselves or the company at risk.

## LEADERSHIP IN ACTION: OWNING THE GRAY

During a complex file review, Julia noticed a misapplied endorsement that had resulted in an underpayment. The issue wasn't caught by QA, and technically, the documentation was complete. But she hesitated.

Instead of allowing it to pass, she escalated the issue. The result: a revised payout, a difficult conversation, and a grateful policyholder who said, "Thank you for making it right."

When her team asked why she spoke up, Julia simply said, "We don't hide errors. We fix them. That's who we are."

Her example became the foundation for a new team principle: prioritizing accuracy over avoidance.

## Building Systems That Reinforce Ethics

As a leader, you cannot assume your team knows how to apply compliance in every scenario. You must establish systems for consistency—clear file handling expectations, standards for policy interpretation, and strong documentation habits. Additionally, you should cultivate an environment where asking questions is not a weakness but a strength; where ethical concerns are welcomed, not feared; and where doing the right thing is expected—not exceptional.

And yet, ethics rarely present with flashing warning signs. They often manifest in subtle decisions: the temptation to close a file quickly instead of thoroughly, the inclination to withhold uncomfortable information from a policyholder, and the pressure to meet cost targets that quietly nudge someone away from fairness. It's in these moments that your leadership is most needed.

## Navigating the Gray With Care

Leading ethically doesn't mean you'll never feel torn; it means you're willing to pause, ask questions, and involve others in the decision-making process when the path isn't clear. It involves recognizing that legality and morality don't always align perfectly and that part of leadership is navigating that tension with humility and care.

It also means protecting your culture. When ethical lapses go unaddressed, even minor ones, they send a message: speed matters more than truth. Numbers matter more than people. But when ethical choices are celebrated—when someone speaks up about an inconsistency and is thanked, not silenced—it changes everything. It reinforces that values aren't just words on a wall; they're real, and they're lived.

## The Ethical Burden of Technology

In times of pressure or uncertainty, your team will look to you. Not for answers to every policy nuance or legal statute—but for steadiness. For reassurance that values come first. That they can trust the process because they have faith in the people leading it.

As technology introduces new tools and AI increasingly influences decisions, ethical leadership becomes critical. While automation can enhance efficiency, it can also create distance. A decision made by an algorithm still affects a real person, and someone—some leader—must remain responsible for ensuring that the decision is fair.

## Leading With Principle

In the end, ethical leadership isn't about being perfect; it's about being principled. It involves taking responsibility when you fall short and recommitting to the standard you want to uphold. It focuses on leading with clarity when others are unsure and protecting what matters most—not just the claim, but the people behind it.

Leadership in insurance adjusting is already demanding. However, when it is rooted in ethics, it transforms into something greater. It becomes a force for trust, fairness, and long-term impact.

## 🔭 Looking Ahead

In the next chapter, we'll explore what it truly means to lead in a way that leaves a lasting legacy. Beyond managing tasks or meeting quotas, legacy leadership is about the influence you have on people's growth, the culture you help shape, and the standards you model even when no one is watching. Whether you're leading a team, mentoring a colleague, or rebuilding after a mistake, your choices leave behind more than results—they leave an imprint. Let's dive into how to lead with that long-view mindset, and why your legacy begins in the everyday moments you may be overlooking.

---

### 🔍 Leadership Reset Prompts — Chapter 14: Ethical Leadership and Regulatory Compliance

*Use these prompts to examine how ethics are practiced—not just taught—within your leadership approach.*

- *When was the last time I paused to ask if the "easy" decision was also the right one?*

- *Have I created safe channels for ethical concerns to surface?*

- *Where have I let ambiguity go unaddressed instead of clarified?*

- *How am I modeling responsibility—not just compliance—for my team?*

---

# Chapter 15

---

## Becoming a Legacy Leader in
## the Insurance Industry

> *"Independent does not mean disconnected. Leadership still matters—*
> *especially when no one is watching."* — Dr. Karissa Thomas

The work of leadership is urgent—but its greatest impact is often invisible in the moment. Day by day, you respond to emails, coach team members, manage expectations, and solve problems that rarely make it into a headline. However, over time, these small, often unnoticed decisions begin to leave a mark. One day, you realize you're not just leading a team—you're shaping a legacy.

Legacy leadership isn't about your title. It's not about how many years you've spent in the field, how many files you've closed, or how many people report to you. Legacy isn't measured by output; it's measured by influence. It's reflected in how people speak your name when you're not in the room, in the systems that continue to work long after you've built them, and in the adjuster who leads well today because you believed in them yesterday.

## Building Legacy in Real Time

In a field as demanding and metrics-driven as insurance adjusting, the concept of legacy can feel distant—like something to consider at the end of your career. However, the truth is, legacy is created moment by moment. It's built in the way you show up in meetings, the tone you use during tough conversations, and the integrity you demonstrate when no one's watching. You don't wait until the end to lead with legacy; you build it now.

For many leaders, this shift begins with a change in mindset. It's no longer about being the one with all the answers; it's about creating space for others to grow, contribute, and rise. It's about moving from being the center of the work to becoming a multiplier of others' capacities. Legacy leaders don't just lead tasks—they lead people into their own leadership.

---

### LEADERSHIP IN ACTION:
### THE VOICE THAT LAUNCHED A CAREER

Michael was a respected file review manager who quietly mentored new hires. During a challenging onboarding cycle, he dedicated extra time to support an overwhelmed adjuster named Rachel.

One day, after she handled a difficult file with grace, Michael simply said, "You're going to lead others one day."

That comment stuck.

Years later, as Rachel led her own team, she shared, "Michael gave me belief before I had results. That's what leadership is."

Michael didn't plan to build a legacy that day. But he did.

---

## Mentorship and Multiplication

That's where mentorship becomes essential. Developing others isn't a bonus role; it's part of your core responsibility. Whether you realize it or not, someone is always observing how you lead. They're learning from your decisions, your patience, your resilience, and even your mistakes. The question isn't whether you're influencing future leaders; it's what kind of influence you leave behind.

You don't need a formal program to begin mentoring. It starts with observation. Who on your team is curious, consistent, or ready for more challenges? Who needs affirmation that their voice matters or clarity on how to grow? Often, the best mentorship comes from conversations that begin with, "I see something in you," or, "Let me walk with you through this." It's simple. It's human. And it lasts.

## Preparing for Succession

Succession planning is another element of legacy that many leaders avoid until it's too late. Preparing others to step into greater leadership doesn't diminish your value—it amplifies it. It signals that you're not just holding space; you're building capacity. Your influence is not tethered to your presence but embedded in the systems and people you've nurtured.

## Culture That Endures

Legacy leadership also involves considering the culture you cultivate. What unwritten norms does your team adhere to because of the example you've set? How do people manage conflict, feedback, or failure based on how you've demonstrated those behaviors? Culture is developed through patterns. It is influenced by what is praised, what is tolerated, and what is overlooked. Moreover, culture, more than any single claim outcome, is what endures.

## Living With a Long-Term Lens

To become a legacy leader, you don't need to change every-thing. You simply need to start living your leadership with a long-term perspective. Ask yourself: what do I want this team to remember when I'm no longer in this role? What habits do I want them to keep? What stories do I want them to tell? These questions guide not just your actions but also your presence.

## Beyond Your Team

And legacy isn't limited to your immediate team; it also involves how you contribute to the profession as a whole. This might include mentoring outside your organization, engaging with indus-try groups, or helping raise leadership standards across the field. In an industry often focused on efficiency and outcomes, leaders who prioritize the human side of the work—empathy, fairness, growth—are desperately needed.

## Leadership That Leaves Something Behind

In the end, legacy is not what you leave behind when you depart. It's what you build while you're here. It's the clarity you bring to your team, the courage you model in uncertain moments, and the belief you offer when someone's unsure of themselves. It's the sense of stability and care that people feel under your leader-ship.

And the beautiful thing about legacy is this: you don't need anyone's permission to start shaping it. You do this every time you choose people over ego, clarity over control, and development over dominance.

## 🔭 Looking Ahead

The next chapter will prepare you to extend that legacy even further—especially when leading teams that may not be composed of full-time staff or on-site colleagues. Leadership isn't defined by location or proximity; it's about vision, alignment, and care—even across distances.

---

### 🔍 Leadership Reset Prompts — Chapter 15: Becoming a Legacy Leader in the Insurance Industry

*These prompts will help you reflect on the influence you're building and the leadership story you're writing every day.*

- *Who on my team might be ready for more responsibility— and how can I support their next step?*

- *What cultural habits have I reinforced through my leadership—intentionally or unintentionally?*

- *If I left this role tomorrow, what would my team carry forward because of me?*

- *What can I do this week to mentor someone in a way that lasts?*

---

# Chapter 16

## Human-Centered Leadership in a Tech-Driven Era

> *"You don't have to be the loudest voice in the room to lead.*
> *Influence often travels in silence."* — Dr. Karissa Thomas

Technology has transformed how insurance adjusting operates. What once required physical presence, paper files, and manual follow-ups now occurs through digital portals, automated triage, virtual inspections, and AI-assisted assessments. In many ways, these advancements have made the work faster, more accurate, and more scalable. However, they have also introduced a subtle risk—one that leaders must now confront head-on.

The risk is this: that in our pursuit of efficiency, we overlook the humanity at the heart of claims work.

A claim is never just data; it's a family without a home, a vehicle totaled in a moment of panic, and a policyholder navigating grief or frustration. It represents a person, often at their worst moment, hoping that someone on the other side of the screen will see them—not just their policy number.

## Leading With People in Mind

Human-centered leadership ensures that technology serves people, not the other way around. It recognizes the power of automation but refuses to allow convenience to replace compassion. It embraces innovation while insisting that ethics, empathy, and critical thinking remain central to every decision.

This begins with awareness. Leaders must understand how new tools impact workflows, customer experiences, and team dynamics. Just because something is digital doesn't mean it is neutral. AI can unintentionally introduce bias. Automation can depersonalize the claims journey. Chatbots can frustrate those who simply want to be heard.

### LEADERSHIP IN ACTION: THE HUMAN REMINDER

When Raylene's team started using an AI-driven triage system, efficiency improved—yet customer complaints about tone and empathy surged. Instead of dismissing it, she had each team member listen to one recorded call per week.

After a few sessions, one adjuster remarked, "I forgot there was a person behind the screen."

Raylene didn't blame tech; she added humanity back into the process. It became their new team mantra: "Efficient, but human."

## Internal Culture and Digital Fatigue

Internally, the same principle applies. As systems become more complex, adjusters can start to feel like cogs—tasked with clicking through screens and hitting benchmarks instead of applying their expertise and building relationships. Human-centered leaders disrupt that pattern. They allocate time for genuine coaching. They foster curiosity. They provide context for the work so that people remember why it matters.

Too often, remote leadership becomes surveillance in disguise. Adjusters working from home report feeling watched—not supported. Every click, call, and delay is logged, measured, and reviewed. What gets lost is the context: the emotional labor behind the screen, the stress no dashboard can detect, and the reality that people are not machines. Human-centered leaders recognize this. They build trust before metrics. They inquire about what cannot be measured. And they understand that performance doesn't improve through pressure—it improves through presence.

## Challenging Tools With Integrity

They also speak up when something doesn't feel right. If a tool is guiding adjusters toward faster closures at the expense of fairness, it should be questioned. If a digital workflow makes documentation easier but undermines customer trust, it should be revisited. Technology should enhance integrity, not challenge it.

Being a human-centered leader doesn't mean rejecting innovation; it means integrating it wisely. It involves asking: "Where does the machine end and the person begin?" And, "What do I want people to remember about their experience with us—not just how fast it happened, but how they felt?"

## Leading Through Tech Transitions

This is especially important in moments of tension. A policyholder who is denied coverage may accept the decision, but only if they feel it was handled with respect and transparency. A frustrated team member regarding a new system may adapt, but only if they feel involved in the learning process and supported throughout the transition.

Human-centered leadership also considers the pace of change. Just because a platform is available doesn't mean a team is ready. Leaders must manage not only the rollout but also the overall experience. Is training accessible? Are expectations clear? Are individuals given the space to learn without fear of failure?

Change fatigue is real. When systems evolve constantly and priorities shift with every tool update, even the best adjusters can feel worn down. Leaders who acknowledge this—who check in, slow down when necessary, and communicate consistently—earn trust. They're not viewed as enforcers of technology but as guides through transformation.

## The Bigger Question

And in a broader sense, this type of leadership is about vision. It focuses on asking: "What kind of claims culture are we building in this digital age?" Is it transactional, automated, and impersonal? Or is it still rooted in service, fairness, and professionalism?

The future of adjusting will continue to evolve. New tools will emerge and processes will develop. However, one thing must remain constant: the belief that people—policyholders, team members, and leaders—are the most valuable assets in this work.

Technology may advance the claim, but it's people who uphold the trust.

## 🔭 Looking Ahead

In the chapters ahead, we'll explore how to scale that trust across teams, systems, and leadership structures—ensuring that even as your team grows, the essence of your leadership remains intact.

## 🔍 Leadership Reset Prompts — Chapter 16: Human-Centered Leadership in a Tech-Driven Era

*Use these prompts to reflect on how you are integrating technology without losing sight of the people behind every interaction.*

- *What new tool or platform have I introduced—and how did I include the human experience in the rollout?*

- *Where might our current use of technology be undermining trust or empathy?*

- *How can I better communicate that adjusters' judgment and emotional insight are still essential?*

- *Am I leading tech transitions with urgency—or with empathy and curiosity?*

# Part 5

## *Leading Modern Claims Teams with Impact*

Claims teams today look different from how they did a decade ago. They are more remote, more diverse, and more complex—operating across time zones, systems, and evolving expectations.

In this section, we shift from mindset to mechanics—equipping you with the tools to lead modern teams in real time. Whether you're managing independent adjusters, scaling systems, or identifying your next wave of internal leaders, these chapters provide a solid framework for leadership that is both strategic and human.

You will explore how to structure your leadership for consistency without rigidity, how to energize teams across digital spaces, and how to sustain your own leadership identity as the pace and pressures of claims work continue to grow.

Leading well today isn't just about keeping up—it's about shaping what comes next.

# Chapter 17

---

## Strategies for Leading Independent Adjusters

> *"Great leaders don't just train skill—they shape belief. Especially when belief is fading."* — Dr. Karissa Thomas

Leading independent adjusters requires a different kind of leadership—one that relies not on organizational hierarchy or daily oversight, but rather on trust, influence, and the clarity that renders distance irrelevant.

You're not managing employees; you're guiding professionals who operate under their own license, often juggling multiple careers, and expect to be treated as partners, not subordinates. This doesn't mean leadership is less important; it means leadership must be sharper—more intentional, more relational, and more deeply rooted in credibility.

### Start With Structure

The first place leadership shows up is in expectations. Independent adjusters don't want micromanagement, but they do need structure. Vague guidelines lead to misalignment, and misalignment leads to friction. If you want independent adjusters to perform well, clarity is your greatest asset. Be specific. Define what "excellent" looks like in your program. Offer examples, not just metrics. Don't assume experience means alignment—assume nothing, and lead everything with precision.

## Relationship, Not Oversight

But structure alone doesn't sustain performance; relationships do.

The best independent adjusters perform for leaders they trust. They respond more quickly, escalate issues sooner, and solve problems without prompting—not because they're under contract, but because they feel connected to the mission and respected throughout the process. That kind of connection isn't built through checklists; it's built through presence.

And presence, in this case, does not mean proximity. It means predictability, responsiveness, and fairness. It involves not only answering questions but also anticipating them. It means saying, "Here's what's coming," or, "Here's what we're seeing in the files," instead of waiting for issues to stack up and cause frustration.

---

### LEADERSHIP IN ACTION: BUILDING TRUST AT A DISTANCE

When Candace launched a new IA program during hurricane season, she implemented weekly emails, a shared Q&A board, and voice note check-ins. One adjuster replied, "You made me feel like I wasn't just a contractor—I was part of something."

The result? Fewer escalations, higher file quality, and a team that agreed to her next deployment.

---

## Culture Without Cubicles

Respect also manifests in the small details: clear payment timelines, streamlined documentation systems, and communication that treats individuals as professionals rather than problems. When an IA has to ask twice for payment, navigate confusing file feedback, or wait days for a simple answer, leadership credibility suffers. In this context, once credibility diminishes, partnership follows suit.

This is why culture matters—even when there's no office, no floor, no water cooler. Independent adjusters still perceive the tone. They communicate with each other. They observe when leaders only appear during problems or when the only feedback they receive is corrective. They notice when a program shifts from being relational to reactive.

To lead a successful IA team, you must invest in culture as though it were a central team—even when it's not.

## Rhythms That Build Loyalty

This means creating rhythms, not just rules. Maybe it's a weekly touchpoint email. A brief video update during storm season. A simple "we see your effort" message when volumes spike. Maybe it's inviting IAs into process improvement discussions. Asking what's working for them—and meaning it. A feedback loop where they feel their experience is shaping the program, not just being used by it.

You don't need constant supervision. You need unwavering respect.

## The Weight IAs Carry

Independent adjusters work tirelessly. They manage chaos and travel frequently. They bear liability and endure the same emotional labor as staff adjusters—sometimes even more. They enter homes after disasters, conveying difficult truths, juggling file uploads at 1am, and balancing a constantly shifting workload. They need leaders who comprehend this reality, not just those who enforce delivery.

And when something goes wrong—and it will—your tone matters more than your title. There's no benefit to leading with shame. Accountability can be firm without being disrespectful. Corrections are more effective when they're specific, fair, and offered in the context of partnership, not punishment.

## Leading the Long Game

There's one more truth often overlooked in this space: leading independent adjusters effectively isn't just about improving performance from contractors. It's about building a reputation in the industry. It's about becoming the kind of leader people want to work with again—on the next CAT, the next program, the next opportunity. Because in the IA world, your name travels. And how you lead doesn't just shape the present team; it shapes who will say yes to you in the future.

So don't just lead for compliance; lead for relationships, trust, and culture.

Because when you do—when you lead independent adjusters not just as file closers but as professionals—you won't have to chase performance; you'll attract it.

## Leading From Within the Firm

Leading independent adjusters within an adjusting firm adds another layer of complexity. Here, you are not just guiding performance—you're representing the firm's reputation, protecting its contracts, and managing the tension between flexibility and structure every day.

Unlike carriers or third-party program managers, IA firm leaders are in the thick of it. You handle the midnight calls. You onboard hundreds during surge season. You track down estimates, address policyholder complaints, and shift between coaching, compliance, and chaos—all while managing relationships with the clients that hired your firm in the first place.

In this environment, leadership is not optional. It's urgent.

## From Field Adjuster to Team Leader

And yet, many firm supervisors emerge from the field without receiving meaningful leadership development. They understand claims. They comprehend fieldwork. However, they have never been taught how to lead a dispersed, diverse, and often rotating team of professionals who aren't technically employees—but still embody your name, your standards, and your culture.

Leadership in an IA firm must be grounded in rhythm and supported by credibility.

You cannot lead by exception; you must lead by example.

## Rhythm Over Reaction

That involves responding to chaos without panic, showing up consistently—even when the storm isn't yours, and holding firm to your firm's standards even when adjusters push back. It means knowing your team by name, not just by number, and asking for quality without breaking people under unrealistic demands.

These teams often feel forgotten—stuck between program rules and policyholder pressure. A good IA firm leader becomes the anchor. You translate guidelines into workflows, decode vague client expectations into real-time decisions, and push for adjuster support while also protecting your firm's reputation.

> ### LEADERSHIP IN ACTION: FROM STORM TO STABILITY
>
> At the end of a challenging hail deployment, Elijah—a firm supervisor—held a team debrief on Zoom. He opened by saying, "We didn't get everything right. But you showed up. You adjusted under pressure. And because of that, the carrier extended our contract."
>
> One IA replied, "That's the first time I've felt thanked after a deployment."
>
> From that point forward, Elijah turned post-deployment debriefs into a ritual. He didn't merely manage performance; he fostered connection.

## Reputation as Strategy

The best IA leaders understand how to balance empathy for the adjuster with accountability for the outcome.

They lead in real time—with voice notes, coaching calls, late-night "you've got this" texts, and early-morning check-ins before work begins. They understand that leading a CAT roster is not about control; it's about rhythm. It's about being predictable when nothing else is.

And when things break—and they will—it's about leading the recovery as intentionally as you led the surge. Did people feel safe raising their hands? Did they feel recognized for their efforts? Were they corrected with clarity, not shame? Were lessons debriefed and systems improved?

These questions aren't just about retention—they're about reputation. Because in the IA world, adjusters talk. They remember who helped them succeed—and who threw them to the fire. Your leadership becomes your recruiting strategy. The way you lead now shapes who will say "yes" next time.

## Holding the Mission

So, whether you're a field leader guiding a handful of adjusters or a regional lead managing hundreds, remember this:

You aren't just managing workflows; you are managing human energy in one of the most demanding professions there is.

Your leadership determines whether people burn out or rise, whether they turn in their work or own the mission, and whether they disappear after this deployment or show up stronger for the next one.

This represents the work of a leader within an IA firm. When executed with consistency, clarity, and care, it not only delivers claims but also cultivates a positive culture.

## Looking Ahead

As technology continues to transform our industry, the way we lead must also evolve—especially when managing decentralized, independent claims teams. In the next chapter, we will explore the unique dynamics of leading independent adjusters and discuss how to foster connection, accountability, and consistency in teams that operate beyond traditional structures.

## 🔍 Leadership Reset Prompts — Chapter 17: Strategies for Leading Independent Adjusters

*These prompts are designed to strengthen your leadership presence, rhythm, and reputation with independent teams.*

- **Where could I bring more structure without overstepping into control?**

- **When was the last time I showed up for my IA team outside of a correction?**

- **What rhythms or rituals can I introduce to build culture at a distance?**

- **How is my leadership reputation shaping who says "yes" next time?**

# Chapter 18

---

## Building Scalable Leadership Systems

> *"You don't need to be favored to lead with integrity. Favoritism changes, but character remains."* — Dr. Karissa Thomas

As your team grows, so does the complexity of leadership. What once worked informally—a quick check-in, a shared understanding, a hallway conversation—begins to fray as the number of adjusters, files, and functions increases. The pace accelerates. The stakes rise. And suddenly, what used to feel manageable now seems reactive, scattered, and unsustainable.

That's when a critical question arises: can your leadership scale?

Scalable leadership doesn't mean doing more; it means doing things differently. It involves building systems that reinforce your vision without requiring your constant oversight. It entails creating clarity that exists beyond your presence. Lastly, it involves designing structures that empower people rather than hinder their progress.

## Replication Without Dilution

At its core, scalable leadership revolves around replication without dilution. Every team member—whether they report directly to you or sit three layers removed—should understand how decisions are made, how quality is defined, and what the culture expects. That doesn't happen by accident; it occurs through systems.

## System 1: Communication

The first system is communication. As teams grow, the margin for misinterpretation increases. What was once a shared assumption becomes a missed expectation. Without a strong communication rhythm, alignment deteriorates. Scalable leaders create communication structures that are predictable, intentional, and multi-directional. Weekly team syncs, monthly leadership roundtables, and quarterly reviews establish systems that facilitate updates, reflection, and feedback—not just status reports.

## System 2: Feedback

The second system is feedback. In smaller teams, feedback may be organic; however, in larger teams, it needs to be embedded. This requires regular one-on-ones, peer reviews, and scorecard reviews that are linked to both performance and development. Feedback becomes scalable when it is not just a leadership trait but also a leadership tool—one that is taught, modeled, and expected at every level.

## System 3: Documentation

Then there's documentation. Scalable leadership requires that knowledge is not confined to a manager's mind. It must reside in shared resources, training modules, and SOPs that team members can access, update, and contribute to. This enables smoother onboarding, minimizes disruptions during role transitions, and preserves institutional knowledge—regardless of turnover or change.

## System 4: Rituals That Reinforce Culture

Systems also include rituals—team behaviors that reinforce culture at scale. Perhaps it's the way your team opens every meeting with a highlight or closes each week by sharing lessons learned. Maybe it's the monthly recognition thread, the biweekly cross-training, or the annual review of what to leave behind. These moments may seem small, but they become powerful cultural anchors. This is especially true as new people join and wonder, "How do things work around here?"

## Structure Enables, Not Restricts

Structure, when executed effectively, doesn't stifle creativity—it liberates it. It eliminates ambiguity, allowing people to concentrate on value. It reduces confusion, preventing energy from being wasted. Moreover, it ensures that regardless of how large the team becomes, the leadership experience remains intentional, supportive, and consistent.

## Capacity Over Control

But scalable leadership isn't just about efficiency—it's about capacity. It represents the difference between a team that relies on your direction at every turn and one that can operate, evolve, and even lead in your absence. This occurs only when you trust others to take ownership and provide them with the tools and authority to do so.

Delegation becomes a leadership discipline in this space, not merely a way to offload tasks but a method of developing others. You're not just assigning work; you're building confidence, exposing people to decision-making, and helping them grow into leaders themselves. When done well, delegation creates depth and multiplies leadership across your team.

---

### LEADERSHIP IN ACTION: REPLICATING CULTURE

When Janelle's adjusting team doubled during a busy CAT season, she feared losing the culture she had worked so hard to build. Instead of trying to personally oversee everyone, she created a guide titled "How We Lead Here." It outlined communication tone, claim quality standards, and how to give feedback.

Her team leads started using the guide during onboarding—and results improved.

"Even when I'm not in the room," Janelle said, "they're leading the way we lead."

That's scalable leadership: when your culture transcends your presence.

---

## Balancing Structure With Presence

As you scale, leadership must shift from personal involvement to strategic influence. You become a culture shaper, a system builder, and a protector of clarity. Your role transitions from doing the work to ensuring that the work can be done—effectively, consistently, and with a shared purpose.

Of course, no system can replace human connection. No tool can automate trust. As you scale, the risk is not just operational; it's relational. People can begin to feel like numbers, cogs, or afterthoughts. That's why scalable leadership also includes time for presence, the occasional phone call, and the quick "I see you" message. The kind of leadership that remembers: structure holds, but relationships grow.

## The Signature of Scalable Leadership

The best systems are those that carry your leadership DNA— your values, your voice, your clarity—into areas where you don't have direct influence. They empower others to act in alignment with your vision, even when you're focused elsewhere. That's scale. That's sustainability. And that's what enables leaders to build something that lasts.

## 👀 Looking Ahead

In the next chapter, we will examine in greater detail how to advance that leadership by identifying and cultivating emerging leaders within your team who can drive the mission even further than you.

---

### 🔍 Leadership Reset Prompts — Chapter 18: Building Scalable Leadership Systems

*These prompts help assess your leadership systems and clarify what needs to evolve as your team grows.*

- *What systems have I built to ensure leadership quality doesn't dilute as we grow?*

- *Where am I still too involved—and where can I empower others to step in?*

- *How are our team rituals reinforcing the culture we want to scale?*

- *What legacy am I building into the systems—not just the outcomes—I'm shaping?*

---

# Chapter 19

## Developing Emerging Leaders Within Your Team

> *"The best leadership moments are often the ones no one sees—but everyone feels."* — Dr. Karissa Thomas

Every strong leader ultimately faces the same question: Who's coming with me?

Not regarding immediate deliverables or performance metrics, but focusing on legacy, capacity, and who will continue to carry the culture forward when you leave the room.

Developing emerging leaders is one of the most important—and most overlooked—roles of a claims manager. It's not just about mentoring the most vocal person on your team or promoting the one who closes the most files. It's about identifying influence before it has a title. It's about building a pipeline of professionals who don't just follow rules but embody values. And it's about recognizing leadership in the moments when someone steps up—not because they have to, but because they choose to.

## Hidden Leaders, Visible Impact

Every team has hidden leaders. Sometimes they appear as quiet anchors—dependable, unshaken, the people others turn to when the day becomes chaotic. Occasionally, they are the ones asking the tougher questions, challenging processes, or pointing out what others are too distracted to notice. Often, they do not see themselves as "next in line." And yet, they are, if provided with the right support, space, and stretch.

---

### LEADERSHIP IN ACTION: SEEING WHAT THEY DON'T SEE

When Darren noticed that Alisha—a soft-spoken adjuster—often debriefed newer team members after difficult calls, he invited her to co-lead a training.

Her reaction? "I didn't think I was leadership material."

His response: "You've been leading—quietly. It's time others see it too."

That single opportunity unlocked her voice—and shaped the way others showed up.

---

## Intentional Development, Individualized Support

Developing these emerging voices requires intentionality. You cannot lead everyone in the same way. Some people need exposure, while others require encouragement. Some need a challenge big enough to reveal their potential. The role of a leader isn't to mold individuals into carbon copies of themselves; it's to create conditions where others can lead with their own style, voice, and integrity.

Leadership development like that doesn't happen in classrooms. It unfolds in real time.

It happens when you invite someone to shadow you during a challenging meeting—not to observe, but to reflect and ultimately lead on their own. It occurs when you allow a team member to take ownership of a project you typically manage, even if it means guiding them through the learning curve. It happens when you mention their name in spaces they have not yet entered, advocating for their visibility.

## Clarity Over Comfort

Emerging leaders also need the truth, not just praise. They need honest reflections on what's working, what's not, and where they still have room to grow—not as criticism, but as clarity. That clarity is a gift. It says, "I see leadership in you, and I want to help you access all of it."

And yes, it requires patience. You may have to watch them stumble. You may have to answer questions you haven't thought about in years. You may feel the impulse to step in and do it faster. However, the cost of speed is often depth. If you always do it for them, they never learn how to carry it themselves.

Leadership is less about sharing your expertise and more about creating space for others to emerge.

## Adjusting Your Posture

This also means adjusting your leadership posture. When you're developing others, your role becomes less about being the expert and more about being a mirror, a challenger, and a coach who not only teaches skills but also helps unlock identity.

And while it may seem like a long play, it is one of the most strategic moves you can make. Your success will never be determined by how much you accomplished alone; it will be measured by how many people grew because you were willing to believe in them before they believed in themselves.

## Culture That Carries It Forward

A team centered around emerging leaders becomes more agile, self-aware, and resilient. Challenges are addressed from various perspectives. Decision-making enhances. Your influence starts to scale—not through control, but through culture.

This is especially critical in adjusting, where the demands are relentless and the pace is unforgiving. If you're the only one holding the standard, answering every question, or driving every result—your leadership ceiling will be reached quickly. But if you build others to carry the mission alongside you, everything expands.

## Begin Now

So pause and ask: Who on my team needs to be seen right now? Who is ready for more responsibility but hasn't had the chance to show it yet? Who is asking the kind of questions that indicate they're already thinking like a leader?

Then invest in them now, not when things slow down.

Developing leadership in others isn't just good practice—it defines great leaders. It is one of the greatest privileges of your role.

## 🔭 Looking Ahead

In the next chapter, we will turn inward to examine what occurs when your leadership identity begins to shift. Whether you are facing burnout, a career transition, or a deeper call for alignment, you will explore how to lead yourself through uncertainty—and rediscover purpose at the leadership crossroads.

## 🔍 Leadership Reset Prompts — Chapter 19: Developing Emerging Leaders Within Your Team

*Leadership is not only about what you do—it's about what you multiply. In the rush to meet deadlines and manage performance, it's easy to overlook the quiet contributors or wait for someone to "prove" they're ready. But real leadership means creating space for others to rise. As you reflect on how you develop those around you, consider the following:*

- **Who have I overlooked because they lead quietly?**

- **When was the last time I gave someone the opportunity to lead before they were "ready"?**

- **Am I offering honest feedback to emerging leaders—or just affirmation?**

- **What am I doing today that someone else could grow from doing tomorrow?**

# Chapter 20

## When the Spark Fades: Leading Yourself Through Leadership Crossroads

> *"Leadership doesn't end when passion fades—it begins again through purpose."* — Dr. Karissa Thomas

No one talks enough about the quiet moments when leadership shifts from feeling like momentum to feeling like maintenance. When the challenges become repetitive, the passion dulls, and the next step remains unclear. You're not burned out—but you're not lit up either. You're doing the work, guiding the team, and keeping the system moving—but inside, something feels unsettled. It's not failure. It's friction. And it's real.

These are the moments when even the most experienced leaders find themselves at a crossroads.

### The Subtle Signs of Change

Sometimes it starts subtly—a feeling of restlessness, boredom, or emotional fatigue. Other times, it's more abrupt: a restructuring, a missed opportunity, or the realization that you've outgrown the role you once loved. Either way, the question arises: What now?

For many leaders, especially those in the insurance industry, where tenure and loyalty are often regarded as badges of honor, this feeling can be disorienting. After all, you've built something, developed people, and earned trust. Why isn't that enough?

It is sufficient, but it does not mean it is permanent.

## Seasons of Leadership

Leadership, like life, happens in seasons. There are seasons of learning, building, pushing, growing—and seasons of stillness, doubt, or redirection. Feeling stuck doesn't mean you're failing; it means you're human. It might just be the invitation you need to reevaluate what leadership looks like for you now.

Begin with honesty. What do you crave? Is it more creative space, a different type of challenge, reduced operational weight, and increased strategic influence? Is it the opportunity to build something new or simply to feel recognized once more in your current role?

## When You're Carrying Too Much

For many, the frustration stems from feeling unseen by upper management. You're carrying the team, upholding the culture, managing the chaos—yet no one checks on you. No one asks how you're holding up. You're expected to perform without faltering, absorb pressure without complaint, and lead with clarity in an environment that offers little in return. Over time, that weight becomes heavy. Not because you're weak—but because even strong leaders need support.

This is where leadership must also flow upward. Advocate for yourself. Share what's missing. Not every executive understands what it costs to lead well at your level—but they should.

## Maybe It's a Recalibration

These questions don't need to prompt drastic change. Sometimes, what's required isn't an exit but a recalibration.

Perhaps it's a shift in your perspective, a side project that re-engages your energy, or a conversation with leadership about where you wish to grow. Or maybe it's simply a break—a pause to recover from the emotional wear and tear of always being the steady one.

Other times, the answer is broader. Perhaps you're meant to take your experience into a new role, a new company, or a new industry. Maybe you're meant to transition from direct leadership to mentorship, consulting, or thought leadership. Perhaps your next level is less about position and more about purpose.

## Lead Yourself First

There's no single right path—but there is a right approach: listen to yourself. You can't lead others effectively if you neglect your own alignment. You can't model healthy ambition if you quietly silence your own. And you can't expect long-term influence if you constantly force short-term presence in a role that no longer fits.

This isn't about abandoning responsibility; it's about honoring growth. It's about recognizing that the leader you are today may differ from the leader you were five years ago—and allowing yourself the freedom to evolve.

---

### LEADERSHIP IN ACTION: HONORING THE SHIFT

When Jamal began to dread Monday calls—a ritual he once loved—he knew something had shifted. Instead of ignoring it, he journaled his frustrations for 30 days.

What emerged was a pattern: "I miss building. I've become the maintainer."

That insight didn't lead to a resignation—it led to a new proposal. Jamal pitched a stretch project aligned with his strengths—and his spark returned.

He didn't abandon leadership. He reframed it.

---

## Find the Right Voices

If you're at a crossroads, surround yourself with people who won't rush you—people who can ask you good questions, reflect your strengths back to you, and hold space for you to explore without judgment. Avoid individuals who make you feel ungrateful for even asking. Leadership is lonely enough; you don't need shame in the mix.

And most of all, remember that these seasons are not signs of weakness; they are rites of passage. Every great leader has faced them. The only difference is whether they allowed discomfort to push them into denial or clarity.

You may not know the next step today, and that's okay. What matters is that you've started asking. You're listening to the questions beneath the questions, and you're willing to lead yourself with the same grace, honesty, and courage that you offer your team.

Because the truth is leadership doesn't end at the crossroads. Sometimes, that's where it begins anew.

## Looking Ahead

In the next chapter, we pause to explore the often-overlooked side of leadership—the emotional weight, identity shifts, and quiet resilience required to remain grounded while guiding others. You will reflect on your inner life as a leader and discover how emotional wellness and self-awareness shape every external outcome you influence.

## 🔍 Leadership Reset Prompts — Chapter 20: When the Spark Fades: Leading Yourself Through Leadership Crossroads

*Every leader reaches moments when the work that once felt purposeful begins to feel heavy. These seasons are not failures— they're invitations. Invitations to realign, reflect, and reimagine. If the spark is fading, it may be time to listen more deeply to what your leadership path is asking of you next.*

*Use these prompts to reflect on whether your current leadership season still aligns with your deeper values and goals:*

- *What part of my leadership role energizes me—and what part feels like friction?*

- *If nothing changed in the next year, what part of me would be most disappointed?*

- *What honest conversation do I need to have—with myself or with someone else?*

- *• What would I pursue if I allowed myself to imagine a new kind of leadership future?*

# Part 6

## *Emotional Integrity and Culture in Action*

At this stage of your leadership journey, technical skill is no longer the primary concern. The deeper work involves how you lead when no one is watching—how you manage pressure, stand your ground, and shape culture through your presence, not just your process.

This section delves into the inner landscape of leadership: emotional wellness, generational dynamics, unspoken expectations, and the quiet cost of unresolved tension. It emphasizes leading from a place of wholeness—especially when systems feel transactional, and your authority is challenged.

You'll learn how to model emotional steadiness in chaos, address cultural undercurrents that impact performance, and lead with humanity in a measured industry that often overlooks it. Leadership is not just a strategy—it's a mirror. It reveals who we are, and it shapes who others become under our influence.

These final chapters concern not only what you do as a leader but also who you choose to be.

# Chapter 21

---

## The Inner Life of a Leader — Emotional Wellness, Identity, and Resilience

> *"You cannot restore what you won't acknowledge. Trust is rebuilt through truth, not tactics."* — Dr. Karissa Thomas

There is an aspect of leadership for which no one prepares you: the internal work.

The moments when the weight of decision-making lingers for hours. The pressure to hold it together while your team struggles. The silent recalibration that occurs as your identity begins to evolve—no longer just the doer, but now the guide. No longer the one who executes, but the one who carries others. These topics are not found in standard leadership development programs, yet they are the most defining.

Because behind every confident leader, there lies a very human story.

### Emotional Demands of Leading

Leadership, especially in a high-stakes, high-volume field like insurance adjusting, can often feel emotionally demanding in ways that aren't easy to articulate. There is a constant need to shift between empathy and efficiency, along with the burden of navigating systemic pressure while trying to protect your team. Moreover, there is the loneliness of being the person others depend on—but who may not feel supported in return.

Over time, this can lead to quiet erosion—not necessarily burnout, but something subtler: a detachment, a dulling of motivation, and a sense that, while the work still matters, something inside you feels tired. If left unexamined, that tiredness can begin to shape how you lead, how you show up, and how you perceive yourself.

## Wellness as a Leadership Practice

This is why emotional wellness should be integral to leadership practices.

It begins with self-awareness: recognizing the emotional residue that difficult conversations leave behind, noticing when your patience is fraying more quickly than usual, and acknowledging when your sense of purpose has dimmed. These are not signs of weakness; they are signals—indicators that your internal world needs tending.

Leaders often prioritize the well-being of others. However, sustainable leadership requires a rhythm of reflection. It's essential to ask yourself challenging questions: What am I holding right now that's not mine to carry? What am I avoiding that needs my attention? Where do I feel disconnected—from my team, the mission, or myself?

> ## LEADERSHIP IN ACTION: RETURNING TO ALIGNMENT
>
> After overseeing a record-breaking deployment, Simone began to notice a short temper, difficulty sleeping, and a lack of joy in her work. While her productivity hadn't dropped, her presence had.
>
> She took a one-week break—not to escape, but to reflect.
>
> She returned and made one small change: every Friday, she blocked an hour to journal. Her entry prompt? "Where did I lead from alignment this week—and where did I lose it?"
>
> The answer was never perfect. But the pattern gave her clarity. Her team noticed—and so did she.

## Reclaiming Yourself

Sometimes the answers are practical. You need better boundaries, more support, and a moment to step back and recalibrate. But at other times, the answers run deeper. Occasionally, you find yourself wrestling with who you've become in this role. Maybe leadership has asked you to be more structured, more diplomatic, and more performance-focused—and in the process, you've lost touch with that part of you that once felt grounded and instinctual.

That's an identity shift, and it's normal; however, it requires attention.

Your role may have changed, but your core doesn't have to. You can lead with structure and still be intuitive. You can hold people accountable and still lead with softness. You can adapt to the demands of the work without allowing it to reshape your sense of self.

However, to achieve this, you must frequently and deliberately reconnect with yourself.

## Your Health Is Not Optional

Make space in your week for what anchors you—whether it's walking, journaling, faith, stillness, or creative expression. Treat it as maintenance, not indulgence. The leader your team needs is not the one who can work the longest hours; it's the one who is most emotionally regulated, most self-aware, and best able to lead from a place of integrity instead of exhaustion.

This work is personal, but it isn't solitary. Find people with whom you can be real: a mentor, a peer, a coach—someone who understands the complexity of leadership and can hold space for the moments when you don't want to be "on." You do not have to carry this alone; you were never meant to.

## Redefining Resilience

Resilience is not about pushing through at all costs; it's about learning to return to yourself after being stretched. It involves releasing what isn't yours, repairing what's frayed, recommitting to what still matters, and doing it again—without losing yourself in the process.

Leadership will always demand something from you. However, it should never cost you your health, clarity, or wholeness. You are not just a leader; you are a person leading, and your humanity matters.

## The Heart of the Work

If there is one truth that connects this entire book, it is this:

Leadership is emotional work. You deserve to lead in a manner that honors both the mission and the person behind it.

That is your true legacy.

## 📯 Looking Ahead

In the next chapter, we will explore how generational differences shape communication, expectations, and leadership dynamics within claims teams. You'll learn to lead with empathy across age groups, bridge cultural and experiential gaps, and create a workplace where every generation feels valued, heard, and aligned.

---

### 🔍 Leadership Reset Prompts — Chapter 21: The Inner Life of a Leader — Emotional Wellness, Identity, and Resilience

*Behind every decision, every directive, and every meeting is the inner world of a leader—one that often goes unseen. Leadership is not just external; it is deeply internal. If you neglect that inner life, the outer performance eventually suffers. These prompts are an invitation to check in with yourself—not your role, your results, or your team—but you.*

*Use them to center your emotional well-being, personal identity, and internal leadership rhythm:*

- *Where do I feel misaligned in my leadership today—and what is that telling me?*

- *What practice could I start this week to nurture my emotional clarity?*

- *Who in my life supports the person behind the leader—and have I reached out?*

- *How can I give myself the same care I extend to my team?*

# Chapter 22

## Leading Across Generations in Claims Teams

Step into almost any claims department today, and you'll find a blend of generations working side by side—Baby Boomers who have navigated decades of industry evolution, Gen Xers who have often served as the stabilizing force of leadership, Millennials who have emerged as process-minded contributors and culture-shapers, and Gen Z professionals entering the field with urgency, questions, and unapologetic expectations for clarity and care.

It's one of the most dynamic aspects of leadership today and one of the least discussed.

### Misalignment, Not Malice

For leaders, this multigenerational landscape isn't just interesting; it's layered and, at times, challenging to navigate. Not because generations are inherently in conflict, but because each one has been shaped by a different narrative of what work is, how leadership should function, and what professionalism looks and sounds like.

These stories appear in subtle ways.

A Baby Boomer who prefers emails over Slack messages may be viewed as resistant to change. A Gen Z adjuster who asks "why" before complying could be seen as disrespectful. A Millennial leader introducing new systems might encounter silence or hesitation from team members who have witnessed many "initiatives" come and go. But beneath the tension lies not entitlement or defiance—it's misalignment.

Misalignment can be fixed.

## Lead by Noticing, Not Knowing

Leadership in a multigenerational environment isn't about knowing everything. It's about noticing. It involves becoming the kind of leader who sees the layers beneath behavior, translates experiences, and honors differences while still holding the team to a shared standard.

To do this well, you must lead with both emotional awareness and practical skills. Generational leadership is not about fixing people; it's about connecting with them. This connection doesn't begin with assumptions; it begins with curiosity.

What motivates this person? What does feedback mean to them? How do they define fairness? What do they need from me that they may not know how to ask for?

These questions are not easy. They help keep your team aligned when the pressure is on.

## Stereotypes Aren't Strategies

It's easy to fall into generational shorthand, but stereotypes aren't strategies. You've likely heard or thought these before—Boomers are rigid, Gen X is disengaged, Millennials are sensitive, and Gen Z is entitled. None of that reflects leadership language. Leadership poses a different question: What's the need beneath the behavior?

A tenured adjuster might resist a new platform not out of resistance to innovation, but because they've already adapted to five systems in the last decade and understand the cost of transition. A younger adjuster might seek frequent feedback, not due to a lack of confidence but because they've grown up in a culture that values responsiveness and engagement. A Gen X manager might delegate with minimal follow-up not out of distance but from a deeply held belief in autonomy and trust.

## Flexible Leadership, Firm Standards

As a leader, your role is not to take sides. It's to cultivate a rhythm where all of those truths can coexist and where your leadership can flex without fracturing.

This doesn't mean over-catering. You don't have to become four different people to lead a multigenerational team. What you need is presence, adaptability, and the willingness to adjust your communication tone when necessary, without compromising your core values.

Sometimes, this means delivering feedback in different ways. For a newer adjuster, it might sound like: "Here's what I appreciated about your approach, and here's how we can sharpen it together." For someone more seasoned: "This pattern has come up before—I trust you'll know how to correct it." Both are clear and respectful, but each is delivered in a way that meets the person where they are.

## Clarity Is the Common Ground

Clarity serves as the common denominator. Regardless of the generation, people crave certainty about expectations. Ambiguity, rather than age, is the true cause of disengagement. When expectations are clear, accountability is shared. Furthermore, when accountability is modeled—not just enforced—people engage differently, regardless of their age or how long they have been in the role.

## Storytelling and Reverse Mentorship

One of the most powerful tools for bridging generations is storytelling. Not scripted corporate values, but real stories. They tell how the team handled that surge event, how an adjuster navigated a tough policyholder call with grace, and what worked—and what didn't—in times of pressure. Stories are universal, and they help humanize experience across age and role.

Equally powerful is creating moments of reverse mentorship. Pair younger adjusters with senior colleagues for case reviews, then switch roles for tech tips or to brainstorm ideas. This builds mutual respect—not by mandate, but through experience.

---

### LEADERSHIP IN ACTION: TRANSLATION OVER TENSION

During a team debrief, a senior adjuster interrupted a Gen Z colleague who was proposing process changes. The room became tense.

Rather than take sides, Maya— the team leader—stepped in: "I think what we're seeing is two perspectives with the same goal. One sees risk in change. The other sees risk in staying still. Let's look at what matters most to the process—not just who's right."

The tone shifted. Ideas resumed. That's leadership in action: translation over tension.

---

## Lead the Blend

And when tension inevitably arises, leadership becomes translation. Not defense, not dismissal—translation. "I know that came across as abrupt, but I believe they were trying to move quickly in a high-pressure moment." Or, "Let's take a second to step back—I hear two valid perspectives here. Let's get clear on what matters most."

That's what it means to lead across generations: not through perfect fluency, but through humility. By remaining curious when frustrated and recognizing that the future of claims work will require every generation to stay open—not only to change but also to one another.

Because at the end of the day, your team doesn't need uniformity. They require trust. They need leadership that can recognize differences while still believing in the possibility of a shared vision, culture, and excellence.

And they need you to demonstrate that belief— not just once, but each day.

## 🔭 Looking Ahead

In the next chapter, we will turn our attention to the expectations that often go unspoken—but still shape culture, performance, and trust. You'll uncover how silence surrounding standards, boundaries, and communication norms can quietly erode team cohesion—and how emotionally intelligent leaders bring those expectations into the open with clarity and care.

## 🔍 Leadership Reset Prompts — Chapter 22: Leading Across Generations in Claims Teams

*Every generation brings its own set of values, communication styles, and unspoken norms. In high-pressure claims environments, these differences can either fuel collaboration—or create silent divides. The strongest leaders do not avoid these differences; they translate them into trust. Before you manage across generations, pause to reflect on how you're relating, listening, and leading.*

*Use these prompts to better connect, communicate, and collaborate across generational lines:*

- *Where am I using assumptions instead of curiosity?*

- *What expectations have I failed to clarify across the team?*

- *Who on my team could benefit from reverse mentorship— and how can I make it happen?*

- *When generational tension shows up, do I translate—or take sides?*

# Chapter 23

## The Cost of Unspoken Expectations

The toughest conversations in leadership aren't always the ones you engage in; they're often the ones you never had.

Not every misstep on a team results from resistance. Sometimes, it stems from confusion. Other times, it arises from assumptions. Often, it's silence where clarity should have existed. Too frequently, the expectations that reside silently in a leader's mind become the fault lines beneath team tension.

### Misalignment in Disguise

Unspoken expectations incur a cost. They create misalignment, frustration, and quiet disengagement. A team member may believe they're succeeding when they're actually falling short. Alternatively, they might meet the visible target while missing the invisible standard. Over time, this gap fosters resentment. You wonder why someone "doesn't get it." They wonder why you're never satisfied.

The truth is that most people want to do good work. They want to be respected and to grow. However, they can't meet expectations they don't understand. When feedback is vague or entirely missing, they fill in the gaps with fear or apathy.

## In Adjusting, Ambiguity Has a Cost

In insurance adjusting, where precision and compliance are non-negotiable, ambiguity becomes especially dangerous. A missed expectation can lead to errors, missed timelines, and reputational risk. Furthermore, it can also trigger something deeper: the erosion of trust.

Clarity is not micromanagement; it is leadership. It involves taking the time to slow down, make your standards visible, and explain the reasons behind them. It entails clearly defining what success looks like and how you will measure it. Furthermore, it requires a willingness to revisit those expectations as the team evolves.

## Operational and Relational Expectations

But expectations are not just operational; they are relational. Do your team members know how you prefer to receive updates? Do they know when to escalate an issue versus handle it independently? Do they understand what earns your trust—or unintentionally weakens it?

When these things are left unnamed, people tend to guess. And guessing is where teams fall apart.

---

### LEADERSHIP IN ACTION: ONE ASSUMPTION TOO MANY

When Mark noticed repeated missteps in documentation, his first instinct was frustration. But rather than reprimanding the team, he paused and asked, "What do you think 'detailed notes' means to me?"

The answers varied wildly.

That moment changed everything. He created a sample file, broke down expectations, and offered real-time coaching. Errors dropped—and so did team tension.

He didn't lower the standard. He finally made it visible.

---

## Clarity and Curiosity Go Together

As a leader, your clarity sets the tone, but your curiosity does too.

When someone underperforms, ask: "Was I clear about what was expected here?" When someone surprises you—in a good way or a bad way—pause and reflect: "What assumption was I holding that needs to be clarified moving forward?"

Clarity secures your culture.

And just as importantly, it protects your team's confidence. When individuals know the target, they can aim better. When they trust that your feedback is linked to a shared understanding—not a moving goalpost—they stop trying to read your mind and start focusing on growth.

So, clarify your expectations. Ask what they understood. Align before delegating tasks.

And remember: some of the most expensive mistakes are not made out of defiance but out of silence.

## Looking Ahead

Next, we explore what occurs when your leadership is directly challenged. In high-pressure environments, authority can be tested in subtle or overt ways. The next chapter will demonstrate how to lead with integrity, maintain your ground without ego, and exemplify steadiness when your influence is questioned.

## 🔍 Leadership Reset Prompts — Chapter 23: The Cost of Unspoken Expectations

*The most overlooked form of miscommunication is not what's said—but what's assumed. When expectations remain unspoken, even strong teams can falter. What feels obvious to you may be unclear to others. As a leader, clarity is not just a skill—it is a responsibility. Before you evaluate performance, take a moment to evaluate your communication.*

*Use these prompts to revisit and reinforce the clarity of your leadership:*

- *What expectations have I left unspoken that may be contributing to team tension?*

- *How am I confirming—not assuming—that we're aligned before delegating?*

- *Have I made both my operational and relational expectations visible?*

- *When someone misses the mark, do I ask if clarity—not just effort—was the issue?*

# Chapter 24

## Holding the Line: Leading with Integrity When Your Authority is Challenged

There's a moment every leader faces, although few admit it. A moment when your voice is dismissed in a meeting. When your decision is challenged behind your back. When you offer direction—and someone disregards it without hesitation. You try to remain calm, professional, and objective. But something about the moment stings.

Not because you need control, but because you've earned your seat—and now it feels like someone's pulling it out from under you.

### Subtle Undermining

Leadership involves not only guiding others but also maintaining your composure when they doubt, question, or quietly oppose you. In the realm of insurance adjusting—where leadership is often fast-paced and closely scrutinized—these moments occur more frequently than we may like to admit.

Being undermined is not always loud; sometimes it's subtle. A team member "forgets" to loop you in, a colleague corrects you publicly, and a higher-up reassigns your directive without discussion. These actions don't just create friction—they foster internal questioning. You begin to ask: Am I being too passive? Too direct? Too inexperienced? Too much?

The hardest part isn't the behavior itself; it's what it awakens within you. That's where the real leadership work begins.

## Responding Without Reacting

When you're second-guessed or ignored, your first instinct may be to defend yourself, assert your title, or tighten your grip. However, leadership grounded in ego often falters under pressure. Instead, you must learn how to hold the line—with clarity, calm, and integrity.

Holding the line doesn't mean proving your power; it means preserving your presence. It means staying grounded when others are reactive. It means refusing to be baited by passive resistance and choosing instead to lead from your center, not from your frustration.

There are moments when silence is powerful and instances when it conveys permission. Strong leaders recognize when and how to intervene.

## Language That Restores Respect

When someone disregards your direction, respond with clarity: "I want to revisit what we aligned on—because this shift created confusion, and I want to reset expectations." When your role is questioned in a group setting, re-anchor: "For the sake of clarity and accountability, let me summarize the approach I'm leading here." When your influence is being chipped away behind closed doors, address it directly: "I'd like to understand where the breakdown in communication is coming from. Let's realign—respectfully."

These conversations are uncomfortable. However, avoiding them won't safeguard your leadership; it will diminish it.

> ### LEADERSHIP IN ACTION: CALM UNDER CHALLENGE
>
> During a stakeholder call, a partner publicly second-guessed Jonah's decision. The room fell silent.
>
> Instead of reacting, he paused and said, "Let's pause for alignment. I'd like to walk everyone through the rationale here so we're working from the same context."
>
> The energy shifted. Defensiveness deflated. Clarity returned.
>
> He didn't defend his role—he demonstrated it.

## The Cost of Silence

Every time you let a challenge go unchecked, you teach people how to treat you. Over time, your silence signals that others can disregard your guidance without facing any consequences.

But how you respond is as important as whether or not you respond.

The goal is not to instill fear; instead, it is to restore clarity.

Leadership based on intimidation isn't true leadership—it's merely insecurity in disguise.

## Reflect Before Reacting

At the same time, leaders must be honest with themselves. Is the resistance rooted in disrespect, or in a lack of understanding? Are people pushing back out of defiance, or because they have never been invited to understand the reasoning behind your decision?

Leadership isn't about being liked; it's about being trusted. Sometimes, trust is built not by asserting your voice louder, but by inviting others to speak so you can address what is unspoken.

This doesn't mean surrendering your authority; it means exercising it in a different way. Power is loud, while influence is steady.

## When the Pain Comes From Within

You may not always win people over. However, when your words align with your actions, when your decisions are principled rather than reactive, and when your leadership remains consistent even under pressure, you earn credibility.

Credibility is what endures.

It's also worth noting that being undermined hurts more when it comes from within—when it's your own team, your peers, or someone you mentored. In those moments, it's tempting to personalize the behavior and see it as a reflection of your worth.

But it is not.

Other people's immaturity, ego, or fear does not mean you're failing as a leader. It indicates you're in a moment that requires more from you—not to shrink, but to rise. To reaffirm your voice. To lead without apology. And to remember that leadership is not validated by how others treat you, but by how you choose to show up when they don't.

## Lead Without Apology

Sometimes, leadership can feel lonely. However, feeling lonely doesn't mean being lost.

You don't have to tolerate disrespect silently, nor do you have to respond to it with aggression. There is a third path: the path of a firm, clear, values-rooted presence.

Stand your ground. Not because you need to win, but because what you're building—the culture, the trust, the team—is worth protecting.

That's leadership. Not when it's easy. But when it's tested.

And when you can hold the line without losing yourself, that's when you know you're not leading for approval; you're leading for impact.

## 👀 Looking Ahead

In the final chapter, we bring the conversation full circle—reaffirming the power of human-centered leadership in an industry that often prioritizes speed and structure over empathy and presence. You will explore how to lead with both results and compassion, ensuring that your impact is measured not just by what gets done, but by how people feel under your leadership.

## 🔍 Leadership Reset Prompts — Chapter 24: Holding the Line

*Some leadership challenges do not arrive loudly—they creep in quietly through passive resistance, subtle undermining, or the silence that follows your decisions. Holding the line requires discernment, not defensiveness. It means protecting the culture without sacrificing your core. These prompts are designed to help you lead with conviction when your leadership is quietly tested.*

*Use them to check in with your boundaries, responses, and presence under pressure:*

- *Where am I tolerating subtle disrespect that requires a clearer response?*

- *How do I differentiate between healthy pushback and hidden undermining?*

- *What is one phrase I can practice to restore clarity in the face of quiet resistance?*

- *How can I show up with integrity, even when others don't?*

# Chapter 25

## People First — Leading with Humanity in a Measured Industry

Insurance adjusting is a business of precision—of deadlines met, files closed, and metrics reviewed. The numbers are everywhere: cycle times, QA scores, contact windows, dollar averages, and audit outcomes. At any moment, your performance—or that of your team—can be translated into data points. It is tempting to believe that what gets measured is what matters.

But numbers don't tell the whole story. They never have.

No metric reflects the emotional weight of telling someone that their roof damage is not covered. No spreadsheet accounts for the energy it takes to stay calm when a policyholder screams, pleads, or sobs on the other end of the phone. No scorecard captures the emotional labor of managing back-to-back losses, dealing with ambiguity, or absorbing blame for a system you didn't design.

### The Pressure to Perform

Still, the pressure remains: perform or be penalized. Meet the metric or face the consequences. In some environments, even pay becomes conditional—held over adjusters' heads like a leash, tethered to a narrow definition of "good performance." The result is a culture of survival, not ownership. People work not from pride but from fear. And fear never produces sustainable excellence.

Performance incentives, when used effectively, can inspire. However, when employed as threats, they erode trust. Leadership must recognize the difference. Fear may ignite urgency, but it cannot maintain motivation. Genuine performance flourishes in environments of trust, clarity, and emotional safety.

We are not managing machines; we are leading people. People cannot thrive in cultures that treat them as parts in a production line.

## Culture or Compliance?

Surveillance programs, constant monitoring, and algorithmic scoring systems may promise efficiency, but they also erode trust. Adjusters begin to question whether they are valued for their skill—or simply for their statistics. When trust breaks, initiative disappears. Creativity evaporates. People learn to do the bare minimum—not because they don't care, but because care has become a liability in a system that mistakes pressure for presence.

This is the moment when leadership must draw a different line. Not between good and bad performers—but between sustainable culture and silent harm. Between leadership that asks, "Why didn't you meet the goal?" and leadership that asks, "What's getting in your way?" Between environments that demand compliance and those that nurture capacity.

## Humanity Is Not a Luxury

To lead with humanity is not to coddle. It is to create room for people to be whole, to make space for the emotional realities of the work, and to acknowledge that even the best adjuster will have off days, off claims, and off cycles. Grace, not punishment, is often the truest form of accountability.

There must be room to pause without guilt. Room to ask for help without shame. Room to say, "I'm overwhelmed," without wondering if that vulnerability will cost you your contract or your raise.

And there must be room for leaders to be human, too.

## Leadership Cannot Be Sustained in Isolation

Because leadership in this industry is often lonely. The pressure doesn't disappear—it multiplies. You're expected to carry your team's needs while navigating expectations from upper management. You're asked to be steady for everyone else, even when your own support feels thin. And when you finally admit, "I'm struggling," the response is often, "You'll figure it out."

That's not support. That's abandonment dressed up as autonomy.

Upper management cannot afford to ignore the emotional landscape of leadership. When middle leaders experience burnout, it doesn't just affect output—it impacts culture. It influences retention. It erodes trust throughout every layer of the organization. The ripple effects are measurable, even if the causes are not.

## What the Industry Needs Now

If we want adjusters to perform, we must honor their humanity. If we want leaders to lead well, we must support them beyond the numbers. If we want organizations to thrive, we must stop pretending that emotional labor is an extra.

People are not files. They are not dashboards. They are not quality scores. They are human.

And human leadership—leadership that listens, pauses, stays curious, and resists the urge to control—is not a soft skill. It is a survival skill in a culture that often forgets what makes this work worth doing.

## Leading With Heart

Performance matters. But people matter more.

And when leadership starts there—when it begins with presence, not pressure—it not only builds better teams,

It builds trust. It builds loyalty. It builds legacy.

Because the goal isn't perfect production. The goal is sustainable excellence—rooted in care, grounded in humanity, and led by people who remember what the work is really about.

Not just the claim. But the claimant. Not just the task. But the team. Not just the numbers. But the names behind them.

That's what people-first leadership looks like. That's what this field needs now. More than ever.

## LEADERSHIP IN ACTION

Kendra, a seasoned team lead at a national adjusting firm, had always been known for her speed and accuracy. Her metrics were solid, and her team's numbers consistently met or exceeded expectations. But when two of her top adjusters suddenly began missing targets, the pressure from upper management was immediate: correct the issue or face consequences.

Instead of defaulting to warnings and write-ups, Kendra paused. She held individual check-ins with each adjuster—not to interrogate, but to listen. One had recently lost a parent; the other was quietly struggling with burnout after covering a colleague's caseload for months. Neither had felt safe enough to bring it up.

Kendra made a choice. She advocated for workload redistribution, connected them with internal wellness resources, and adjusted expectations temporarily—not as a favor, but as a strategic leadership decision. Within weeks, morale improved. Performance rebounded. And both adjusters expressed a renewed sense of loyalty to the team.

Her results were no longer just numbers on a dashboard—they were humans still standing, still trying, and still engaged. And that was the metric that mattered most.

## 👀 Looking Ahead

As we move toward the conclusion, you'll be invited to reflect on your entire leadership journey—from mindset and communication to resilience, culture, and human impact. This final section provides a blueprint to help you lead with clarity, emotional integrity, and the confidence to claim your place as a transformational leader in the insurance industry.

---

### 🔍 Leadership Reset Prompts — Chapter 25: People First — Leading with Humanity in a Measured Industry

*In a field defined by metrics, deadlines, and deliverables, it is easy to forget that people—not numbers—carry the work forward. The strongest leaders do not abandon excellence; they redefine it. They find ways to lead with both clarity and compassion. These prompts are a chance to pause and ask yourself: Am I building a culture that prioritizes people as much as performance?*

*Use these prompts to lead with courage, clarity, and care in systems often built for speed, not soul:*

- *What message are my policies and practices sending about what matters most—people or performance?*

- *Where have I normalized urgency over wellness?*

- *How can I reintroduce human-centered leadership in a data-obsessed culture?*

- *What does sustainable excellence look like for my team— and what support do we need to get there?*

---

# Conclusion

## Claiming the Lead —
## Your Leadership Blueprint

Leadership in insurance adjusting is not for the faint of heart. It demands emotional stamina, technical precision, and the courage to guide people through high-stakes, high-pressure environments every day. You are leading in a field where details matter, but people matter more—and where every decision, every conversation, and every moment of presence has the potential to shape how someone experiences their work, growth, and future.

Throughout this book, you've explored what it means to lead not only with strategy, but also with depth. You've unpacked the realities of burnout, communication breakdowns, ethical tensions, and cultural misalignments. You've reimagined leadership amidst change—technological, generational, emotional—and you've been invited to hold both responsibility and empathy in the same hand.

You've explored the layers of what strong leadership truly requires in this field: the ability to coach without controlling, to adapt without abandoning your values, and to build sustainable systems that serve not only the workflow but also the well-being of your team. You've considered how to scale trust across independent and remote adjusters, how to foster performance without sacrificing clarity, and how to navigate your own seasons of uncertainty with grace.

In the final chapters, you took it even further.

You examined what it means to lead across generations—to communicate, motivate, and unite a team with different reference points, rhythms, and realities. You learned to confront the cost of unspoken expectations and to speak with clarity where silence used to reside. You were reminded that your leadership will be tested—not just in times of crisis, but in subtle moments when your authority is questioned or overlooked. Additionally, you were given space to reflect on your own emotional health—the inner life of a leader that so often goes unseen yet shapes everything.

What emerges is not a model of perfect leadership. Instead, it represents something more enduring: a grounded, human, intentional approach to leading that aligns your voice, values, and vision.

Claiming the lead in this field involves more than managing volume, performance, or productivity. It requires building something lasting that accommodates people, growth, and change. It entails developing other leaders, communicating across distances and differences, and showing up with presence in a world that often prioritizes speed instead.

It is important to recognize that leadership is not defined by position but by your influence and how you choose to use it.

Great leadership doesn't announce itself. It isn't always visible. Sometimes, it looks like exercising restraint in a tense meeting. Sometimes, it sounds like posing a better question. Often, it's a quiet decision to listen longer, pause before reacting, or advocate for someone whose voice might otherwise be overlooked.

It's easy to measure the tangibles—files closed, costs contained, cycles met. But the truest measure of leadership resides in what's harder to quantify: the adjuster who stayed because you believed in them, the culture shift that occurred because you refused to lead through fear, and the new leader who emerged because you gave them space to grow before they thought they were ready.

Leadership is not always loud; however, it is always felt.

As you move forward—whether by continuing to lead your team, shaping organizational strategy, or evolving into the next version of your leadership—you will encounter resistance, ambiguity, and unexpected pivots. This is the work. This is the gift. Because leadership is not just a title to carry; it's a presence to embody.

Let this be your blueprint—not for how to do everything perfectly, but for how to stay aligned. Let it guide you when the pressure builds, when your voice shakes, and when the decision feels heavy. Let it remind you that your team does not need perfection; they need your presence.

They need your steadiness when the system shifts. They need your empathy when pressure intensifies. They need your clarity when the path becomes complicated. And they need your integrity—every single day.

You are already taking the lead. Every time you choose to coach instead of criticize, demonstrate calm in a crisis, and develop others while continuing to grow yourself, you shape this industry for the better.

This book concludes, but your leadership continues.

Take a breath. Reflect on who you have become. Then step forward—with the full knowledge that your leadership matters more than ever.

Especially now, with rising metrics and humanity feeling at risk, your presence matters more than pressure. Chapter 25 reminded us that we are not machines—we are people leading people. When leadership returns to that truth, everything else begins to align.

# Claim the Lead™ Discussion Guide: Fast Prompts for Real Leaders

---

This guide was created for real-world leaders—not book club participants. We know adjusters and managers don't have hours to reflect, so this tool is designed to spark quick insight, personal application, and short team check-ins when time allows.

Use it during downtime, in huddles, before deployments, or as part of ongoing leadership training. You don't need a facilitator—just a few intentional minutes to pause, align, and lead more clearly.

---

**Suggested Use**

- Review 1–2 prompts on your own before the start of each week.
- Pick one question to open or close a team meeting.
- Use prompts in 1-on-1 check-ins to develop new leaders.
- Keep it simple: no PowerPoints, just better conversations.

---

## Quick Reflection Prompts by Section

### Chapters 1–5: Leadership Foundations
- Where is leadership most needed on my team right now?
- What shift have I made—or avoided—since becoming a leader?
- What kind of culture do we quietly allow?
- What would sustainable performance actually look like here?

### Chapters 6–8: Communication & Connection
- Where are we assuming instead of asking?
- How can I model clear, calm communication this week?
- Are we coaching, correcting—or connecting?
- How are we building trust across distance?

### Chapters 9–12: Motivation & Crisis Leadership
- What's one small win I've celebrated this month?
- What part of our process is exhausting vs. empowering?
- How did we recover after our last high-pressure stretch?
- Am I leading through disruption—or just reacting?

### Chapters 13–16: Future-Focused Leadership
- Are we preparing for change—or just surviving it?
- Have I named my leadership legacy—or am I winging it?
- How can we center people as tech and policy evolve?
- Where do values show up—or disappear—under pressure?

### Chapters 17–20: Culture, Scale, and Self-Leadership
- What habits could scale our leadership, not stress it?
- Who on my team has leadership potential we're overlooking?
- Am I operating from clarity or emotional clutter?
- What part of my role lights me up—and what dims me?

### Chapters 21–24: Emotional Integrity & Influence

- What do I need to stay emotionally steady this week?
- Where have expectations gone unspoken—and caused friction?
- How do I respond when I'm challenged or overlooked?
- Who needs more support than structure right now?

### Chapter 25: Humanizing Leadership in a Measured Industry

- Where have metrics overtaken meaning on my team?
- Have we ever used pay, pressure, or compliance as control?
- What's one way I can lead with presence, not just performance?
- When was the last time someone felt safe to be human here?

---

### Final Leadership Check-In Questions

Use these quarterly or during performance conversations:

- What kind of team do we want to be known as?
- What's one leadership commitment I'm making this month?
- What's one truth this book reminded me about leadership—or myself?

---

## Optional Team Activity: The Legacy Map

Invite each team member to finish this sentence:
"The leadership legacy I want to leave is..."
"...and here's how I will live that out, day by day."
Post them in your workspace—or use them as quiet north stars.

# Source References and Research Foundations

These references supported the development of leadership principles and performance strategies presented throughout *Claim the Lead: Transformational Leadership for Insurance Adjusting Managers*. They also provide foundational material for continuing education (CE) considerations in partnership with carriers, firms, and state-accredited programs.

Liberty Mutual & Safeco Insurance. (2025). *Independent Agents at Work: State of the Workforce Study*. Liberty Mutual Group. Retrieved from https://insuranceindustryblog.iii.org

Spinify. (2023). *Strategies for Retaining Top Talent in the Insurance Industry*. Retrieved from https://spinify.com/blog/strategies-for-retaining-top-talent-in-the-insurance-industry

Gallup. (2022). *State of the Global Workplace Report*. Gallup, Inc. Retrieved from https://www.gallup.com/workplace/349484/state-of-the-global-workplace-2022.aspx

Progressive Insurance. (2023). *Leadership Pipeline and People Development Report*. Internal publication summary referenced in case studies on talent retention. Retrieved from https://www.progressive.com/about/careers

Society for Human Resource Management (SHRM). (2023). *The Case for Coaching: How Manager Training Improves Performance and Reduces Turnover*. SHRM Foundation.

## Bring Efficient Adjuster to Your Organization

Looking to improve leadership, communication, or culture on your claims team?
Efficient Adjuster™ offers:

- Leadership intensives and team development sessions
- CE-eligible training workshops
- Retreats and executive coaching for claims leaders
- Scalable programs for independent adjusting firms, carriers, and CAT teams

Let us help you turn this book into action—and your team into a culture of clarity, trust, and performance.

✉ **Contact:** contact@efficientadjuster.net
🌐 **Website:** www.efficientadjuster.net

### Continue the Journey with Efficient Adjuster™

Leadership doesn't end when the book does. Keep building momentum with additional resources, development sessions, and continuing education opportunities tailored for the insurance adjusting industry.

## Recommended Reading

*Communicate, Connect, and Lead:*
*A New Standard for Insurance Adjusters*
This practical guide by Efficient Adjuster equips professionals with the emotional intelligence and communication tools needed to navigate high-pressure claims environments. Perfect for team reading, onboarding, or as a companion to *Claim the Lead*.
Available on Amazon.

# About the Author

**Dr. Karissa Thomas** is an award-winning author, educator, leadership strategist, and the founder of **Efficient Adjuster™**—a brand committed to elevating the communication, professionalism, and emotional intelligence of insurance adjusters nationwide.

With over a decade of cross-sector experience in education, corporate training, and insurance claims, Dr. Thomas brings a rare blend of emotional fluency and operational insight to the world of adjusting. She has trained professionals across the U.S. and internationally, helping teams navigate high-volume environments, complex policy demands, and emotionally charged claims with greater clarity and confidence.

Her work spans catastrophe deployment, field and desk adjusting, leadership development, and continuing education instruction. She is the creator of the **Claim the Lead™** framework—a practical model for internal leadership and performance resilience, designed specifically for adjusters working in high-pressure roles.

Dr. Thomas holds a Doctorate in Educational Leadership and an Executive MBA. Her expertise in human-centered communication, cultural intelligence, and adult learning principles informs every book, course, and training she delivers.

Through Efficient Adjuster™, she equips claims professionals with the tools, mindset, and language to lead from any seat—because communication is more than a skill. It's a responsibility.